JAMES J

National Magazine Co.

The Spy cartoon of James Braid.

JAMES BRAID

By
Bernard Darwin

B.T. BATSFORD LTD

LONDON

© Bernard Darwin 1952
© Lady Darwin, Ursula Mommens and Dr Paul Ashton 1991

First published 1952 by
Hodder and Stoughton Ltd, London

Published in paperback in 1991
with the permission of
the estate of Bernard Darwin
by
B.T. Batsford Ltd
4 Fitzhardinge Street
London W1H 0AH

ISBN 0 7134 6680 4

Printed Great Britain by
Billings Limited
Worcester
for the publishers
B.T. Batsford Ltd

CONTENTS

Foreword

ILLUSTRATIONS

ACKNOWLEDGMENTS

The author and publishers are indebted to Messrs. Methuen & Co. Ltd. for permission to quote an extract from James Braid's *Advanced Golf*; to *Country Life* for the extract from Henry Cotton's *This Game of Golf*; and to Mr. J. H. Taylor and Messrs. Jonathan Cape for the extract from *Golf: My Life's Work*.

FOREWORD

I FIRST met James Braid in 1898, so that I had the happiness of knowing him for fifty-two years and of watching him play and occasionally of playing with him when he was at the height of his fame as a golfer. I felt as if I knew him fairly well but, though one of the most lovable, he was one of the least talkative of men, and I am now very sorry that I did not try harder to wring from him some of his youthful memories. I acknowledge with gratitude the generous help of his two sons James and Harry, of his earliest friend, Ralph Smith, of another intimate friend of his, now the only survivor of his mighty rivals, J. H. Taylor, of Robert McKenzie, one of his first assistants, of Will Brown and Bob Horsburgh who were so long his friends and allies in the shop, and of a number of other friends who are members of the Walton Heath Club. I wish also to thank Mr. Scott, the Editor of *Golf Illustrated*, for so kindly letting me search the files of that journal.

B. D.

CHAPTER I

Earlsferry, 1870-1882

JAMES BRAID was born at Earlsferry or, to be pedantically precise, at Elie in Fife on February 6th, 1870. On the 9th of May in the same year Harry Vardon was born at Grouville in Jersey and on March 1st, 1871, John Henry Taylor followed at Northam in Devon. It was indeed a great golfing vintage in which the three who were afterwards to be famous all over the world as the Triumvirate, arrived within little more than twelve months of one another. What I think few of us appreciate, even the older of us, is how immensely golf's empire increased in the eighty years of Braid's life. In England, the country in which most of his life was spent, golf was barely known in the year of his birth. Blackheath to be sure had records stretching back into the mists of time, but the members of that club were but a tiny band of the initiated in the midst of a great profane, ignorant world. Wimbledon, where other Londoners played, had just celebrated its first year of existence, and so had the Liverpool Club at Hoylake, later destined to be the outstanding pioneer among British clubs. Westward Ho! was five years older and was already becoming a place of pilgrimage for all the devotees of this strange religion. And, with all due respect to the Old Manchester Golf Club and Kersal Moor, that, as far as England was concerned, was all.

Even in Scotland golf, though an extremely ancient

game, was by comparison with later times not a very widely known or played one, and the golf 'boom' which came in the 'eighties had almost as great an effect on the game in Scotland as in England. I have been studying the directory of golf clubs in the original *Golfing Annual* 1887-8. In that year when the name of James Braid was already beginning to be locally known as a record holder and medal-winner, there were by my reckoning only sixty-six courses in Scotland, and of the clubs that played on them only some thirty-eight or forty had been founded in or before 1870. The *Golfer's Manual*, published thirteen years before he was born, enumerated only seventeen Scottish clubs. No doubt, as the secretaries of some of the clubs were very anxious to point out, golf had been played on their links for many generations, but the clubs themselves were most of them relatively modern. Except in a few places, of which Earlsferry was one, golf was little more than a casual amusement of the people. It was only ten years before 1870 that the Championship Belt had first been played for at Prestwick, by eight competitors all told. There were still fifteen years to wait for the first Amateur Championship at Hoylake.

This then very briefly was the kind of golfing world into which the boy was born. He was the son of James Braid of the parish of Elie and his second wife, Mary Harris of the parish of Kilconquhar. The father is described on his marriage certificate as a ploughman but later became something in the nature of a herdsman with the Bairds of Elie House, and when he died was described as 'Forester (domestic servant).' He had never played golf in his life, a fact which may help to explain his entire lack of sympathy with his son's taking up the game profes-

sionally, to which we shall come later. I began by
saying that James was born at Earlsferry. He always
professed to believe this himself and proudly called
his house at Walton-on-the-Hill by that name.
Since his death however the Town Clerk of the Elie
and Earlsferry Town Council has discovered and
published the fact that the cottage in Liberty Place
where he was born was in fact in Elie by the smallest
possible number of yards. The distinction is now one
of a purely academic patriotism. The two burghs of
Elie and Earlsferry were amalgamated by the Local
Government Act of 1929 and Liberty Place has been
pulled down and a stable built there instead. It was
therefore decided to erect a plaque in James's memory
in the shape of a granite slab in the Town Hall. We
may hope that the question is now peacefully settled
and that Earlsferry has not been robbed of its
illustrious son.

Though the world of golf in general may have been
but a small one in 1870, Earlsferry was a very busy
little golfing world on its own account. If James
Braid senior had never played he must have been one
of the comparatively few citizens who had not. His
son, writing of his boyhood's days in *Advanced Golf*,
declared that a man in Earlsferry who did not play
golf, unless for good and obvious reason, was regarded
as something of a crank, that the children all played
if they could get any kind of ball or club, and that his
own first distinct vision was of himself running about
outside his parents' house, a tiny golf club in hand.
And Earlsferry, for all it was but a small place, was
the home of golfing giants. James told me once that
in his young days it could very nearly—and I think
he meant quite—have played the rest of the world.
He had not been conscious of modelling his style upon

anyone in particular since there were so many good models. I was quoting this remark the other day to his cousin Will Brown who was in his shop at Walton Heath from 1909 onwards, and said, perhaps rather airily, that there must have been some very good players there. 'They were all good players, sir,' was the proud reply.

There were doubtless some who were fine golfers though little known outside their own parish, but there were others who carried the fame of Earlsferry far and wide, in particular the Simpson family, six brothers, headed by Jack and Archie, and the greatest of all, James's cousin and Will Brown's uncle, Douglas Rolland, one of the most famous of golf's uncrowned kings.

How little these village heroes were known outside their own boundaries is shown by a story told by Horace Hutchinson in his *Fifty Years of Golf*. It was after the Spring Medal at St. Andrews, 1884, that a message arrived there asking if any pair would give a game to two stonemasons from Elie. I will go on in his own words: 'Leslie Balfour asked me if I would play against them. I knew I was not in good form, and I do not think that he was either, but still we said we would play them. They came over and seemed very nice young fellows indeed. The name of the one was Douglas Rolland and that of the other Jack Simpson. We had never heard of them before. We continued to think them very nice young fellows until the ninth hole, at which point we were two up. The truth is the masons had not got their hammers going at all. But we did not know that. On the way home we began to doubt whether they were as nice as we had thought. Rolland began hitting the ball to places where we had never seen it hit before, and

Methuen

The finish of the drive. James Braid in his prime.

Simpson so followed up that they were reaching with a drive and an iron holes that it was at that date scarcely decent to approach in this metallic way. They were "gutty" balls, mind, which did not fly away off the irons like the rubber-cores. They finished that round to the good of us, and in the afternoon made us look very foolish indeed.' Poor Horace and Leslie! Malicious friends used to ask them 'What sort of golfers are the stonemasons of Elie? Are they any good?' Nor could they ever find a thoroughly effective answer till the result of the Open Championship at Prestwick appeared later in the year: Jack Simpson first, Douglas Rolland second.

At much about the same time Rolland gained further fame. A challenge was issued from Hoylake from the friends of John Ball backing him to play any amateur a home and home match. It was taken up by Rolland, who finished nine up at Elie and added further to his lead at Hoylake. Another thirty-six-hole match was played between the two next day when John Ball became five up with six to play and then incredibly lost all the last six holes and the match. It was incredible if we remember John Ball as he later became, the man for a forlorn hope who could pull any match out of the fire, but he did not attain that justly earned reputation for some years and was at first the despair of his admirers who knew what was really in him. I have said that Rolland ended nine up at Elie because I find that statement in the books, but one who saw every stroke of the match, C. R. Smith, known to some people as Charlie and to others as Ralph Smith, assures me that Rolland was in fact twelve up, and there I must leave it. And here I must again express my gratitude to Mr.

Smith, James's oldest friend and his best man, himself a very fine golfer, for a long and delightful talk and much information. About a year or so younger than James, he was born in Canada but came to Elie as quite a small boy, and nobody can, I am sure, give so good an impression of the golfing atmosphere that the youthful James imbibed into his system with the winds of Elie.

Being a hero-worshipper myself, I always like to meet another and when Ralph Smith comes to speak of Rolland, he is as good a hero-worshipper as I have ever seen. He is convinced that Rolland was the greatest hitter of a golf ball that ever lived, and clearly he was a most glorious one, with a natural genius for the game, and a great natural athlete who could run or jump or play any game better than any of his neighbours. Withal he was a grand figure of a man, well over six feet, upright as a dart, broad in the chest and, as anyone can see from old photographs, strikingly handsome. Everyone liked him and he liked everyone; in fact he was the perfect example of the man who is nobody's enemy but his own. He had a splendid constitution on which he could and did for years presume, though he tried it too highly in the end, and a hopelessly irresponsible gaiety of disposition which nothing could curb. 'Clubs!' says Ralph Smith. 'Clubs meant nothing to Rolland. He had two or three of them tied round with a bit of string.' Sometimes he had, by all accounts, not even so many, for he was of the cheerful and convivial carelessness of the bandsman in the old *Punch* picture who had not merely lost his railway ticket but had lost the big drum. There are stories of his arriving to play an exhibition match with no clubs at all, borrowing a few from his opponent, the local professional, and then beating the wretched lender into the middle of next week and the course record into the bargain. At one time being at a loose end, he was engaged as a navvy on some big public works near Liverpool and went over on a holiday to meet his friends who were playing in a professional competition somewhere in the neighbourhood. In a rash moment they asked him why he did not play himself and he replied that he had no clubs. He was therefore fitted out with a scratch set and ungratefully won the competition.

I believe that on the day on which he had to play the second half of his match against John Ball he ought to have attended a summons in a local Court in Scotland, due to an affair of gallantry. Since he could not be in two places at once he went to Hoylake and thought it prudent thereafter to stay in England. That is why until 1894, when the Open Championship was played for the first time on an English course, Sandwich, his name is not to be found among the competitors. He had various jobs in England, among others at Rye, Malvern, Limpsfield and ultimately Bexhill. Wherever he went he was loved, admired and forgiven—an irreclaimably dashing dog that nobody could withstand. It is one of the great golfing regrets of my life that I never saw him hit a ball or heard him exclaim as he rejoiced in his own strength, 'Awa she goes, ma bonny bird!' I only once set eyes on him for a moment and he was then an elderly man crippled with rheumatism, a mere shadow of his old tremendous self.

I shall come back to Rolland later when he is drawing near the end of his career and James is beginning his. Meanwhile he has carried me a little too far ahead, so that I must retrace my steps. Yet

I could not for the life of me refrain from introducing him at once, if only to show what fascinating gods had their shrines at Elie, at which the small, impressionable James could worship. And I do not believe that any boy or man ever worshipped golf more devoutly than this one did. He was all his life a reserved man who did not give vent to his feelings, and I think perhaps he would have thought it hardly decent to express the real consuming passion that he had for golf, but a passion it was. The game was his life, his life's work and his life's love, and that is something about him that cannot be said too soon.

For the earliest part of his history I go to his chapter called 'Some Personal Matters' in *Advanced Golf*. Like, I have no doubt, all properly brought up little Earlsferry boys, he could not remember the time when he did not play golf. 'My first dim recollections of anything at all in this world,' he says, 'were of some vague happenings about the time when I was five or six years of age, and they are of my always being about with a miniature golf club in my hand and running about outside my parents' home knocking a ball with it at every chance that presented itself.' In due course he went to school and on my asking Will Brown whether they were schoolfellows, he answered, 'He took me to school.' Brown was some six or seven years the younger of the two and we seem to see a pleasant picture of the vast James aged ten or eleven, leading the recalcitrant five-year-old at once kindly but firmly to his lessons. Every spare moment from school was spent on the links, as a caddie to visitors in holiday seasons, and in serious, self-improving practice at all other odds and ends of times. Ralph Smith assures me that James was never to be seduced from the links by any attraction. There was for Earlsferry boys football, and there was cricket—perhaps rather amateurish cricket—and in the winter skating. They spread their nets in vain; golf was the only thing to live for.

The difficulty about golf was to get any practicable kind of club. The best that could be done was to pick up by good fortune an old discarded head and a derelict shaft and if possible unite them. 'People nowadays,' he says, 'talk about the modern system of socketing the shafts of wooden clubs on to the heads, as if it were a recent invention, whereas the caddies of my generation certainly socketed the shafts of the clubs that they made for themselves in this way, the method being the simplest possible, namely, boring a hole through the head and fastening the shaft in it as tightly as possible.' Five years younger than James was one destined to be a famous club maker, Andrew Herd Scott who was, unless my memory fails me, the first to popularize the socketed as contrasted with the 'scared' or spliced club. It is a tempting theory that Andrew Scott founded these new clubs on those of his childhood, but I am afraid it will not do. The same happy notion was occurring at much the same time to another little boy far away in Jersey, called Harry Vardon.

Here is the process devised by him and his playmates as described by him later in *My Golfing Life*. 'We decided that we must use as hard a wood as possible, and as the wood from a tree which we called the "Lady Oak" was suitable for our purpose, another important difficulty was satisfactorily overcome. First of all we cut a thick branch from the tree, sawed off a few inches from it, trimming this piece as near as we possibly could to the shape of the heads of the drivers of those players for whom we had been carrying. As splicing was impossible, we agreed that we must bore a hole in the centre of the head, to enable us to fix in the shaft sticks. These were made of thorn, white or black, and when they had been trimmed and prepared to our satisfaction we proceeded to finish off our club. To make a hole in the head we had to put the poker in the fire and make it red hot so as to allow the shaft to be fitted in. Then after tightening it with wedges, the operation was complete.'

There was yet another small boy, just a little younger, Willie Auchterlonie by name, who with his young friends at St. Andrews employed a different method. They went in for the splice rather than the socket; saving up broken fragments of old gutty balls and melting them down. With this substitute for glue they united head and shaft as well as they could and bound them together with tarry whipping if they were lucky enough to find any. Here were three boys all destined to be champions and I wonder if the fact that they had to make the best of so elementary an armoury, and improvise both clubs and shots as best they could, helped to make them the players they became. Assuredly they learnt the hard way, and James believed it afterwards to have been the best education. The only other club the boys ever possessed beyond their home-made driver was usually an old cleek with a long and well lofted head, which was servant of all work, lofter, niblick, putter and all.

One great advantage James had at any rate over many other boys: he had plenty of good models to watch and copy, and watching and copying is the way to learn golf. As I said he was not aware of taking any particular model. Rolland, ten years older than him, would have been an obvious one, but apart from the splendid fury of hitting there was in later years no great likeness between them, unless it was indeed that both had a square stance. Jack Simpson, another hero palpably to be adored, had an open stance. He was a fine, long, slashing hitter with a notably fast swing and was said to hit his cleek shots so hard as to batter the head into the shape of a hoop. And then there was Archie Simpson, only four years older than James. Four years make a great difference in boyhood but they do not mark a difference of generation. Archie seemed doubtless a very big dog as compared with a small one, but still he was possible as a companion; he was not wholly godlike and out of reach and he had one of the most graceful swings of all the players of his day.

One quality I fancy all the Elie players had, namely a dashing fearlessness, a joy in going out to take risks and a wonderful power of getting out of the pickles in which their dash occasionally landed them. Mr. Everard, writing in the Badminton volume soon after James had won his first Championship, referred to 'the do-or-die methods so characteristic of the Elie school, of whom, for brilliant recklessness and daring, the late Jack Simpson outvied all the rest. . . . For such a grand player the mistakes he made were numerous; but his power of recovery generally stood him in good stead, and could he have played the more prosaic short game in a manner at all commensurate with his driving and approaching he would have been well-nigh invincible. In scoring he almost always began with a terribly bad hole early in the day, a 9 or 10 in the first three holes being no un- common occurrence for him; but even with this handicap he was generally well up at the finish.' Mr. Everard professed to see in the new Elie

Champion something of this same bravery of splendid
slashing that had distinguished the older school,
though adding that 'perchance Braid tempers his
game with more discretion.' Doubtless he learnt to
do this, but there remained in him just a little of
the noble demon of utterly fearless hitting which made
his game so attractive to watch and occasionally
put his friends' hearts into their mouths.

By the time he was seven or eight and no doubt
big and tall for his age, James was a good boy player
and rather better, as he himself avers, than most of
his contemporaries. The visitors used every year to
give prizes for the caddies to play for, and when he
was eight James endured the joys and agonies of
card and pencil for the first time in the junior caddies'
competition. In those days the Elie course was one
of nine holes, but there were also three holes in
Melon Park that were sometimes added to the round.
It was three times round these three holes that the
small caddies played. James's score was 54 and he
won by twenty strokes from his nearest pursuer.
Precisely how long were the holes in Melon Park I
do not know, but an average of sixes for a boy of eight,
and the modern reader must always remember that
these were gutty days, sounds uncommonly good.

It was an encouraging start in life and led
apparently to promotion to the senior ranks in the
following year. He had now to face more formidable
competitors including Archie Simpson, a giant of
twelve or thirteen, who was set to give him eight
strokes in the handicap. The start was just not big
enough for Archie won by two strokes, James being
second. Next year Archie was presumably too old
or had ceased to carry, and James, who had once no
doubt looked up to him as dwelling on unattainable

heights, found himself on that same pinnacle, rated
proudly at scratch. The competition was now
played over the official nine-hole course and James
won it two years running.

Caddie days and school days came to an end at
much the same time, when the boy was thirteen, and
now arose the question what was to be done with him.
He himself had no doubts at all; he wanted to stick
to golf in one capacity or another. He had dreamed
of being a golfer ever since he was about nine years
old and the famous Jamie Anderson, then Open
Champion for the third consecutive year, came over
from St. Andrews to play in a match at Elie. He
was a player as unlike as possible to the golfer that
James was destined to become. Here was no slash
and splendour of hitting, but rather an undeviating
and heartbreaking accuracy and the resolute eschew-
ing of any form of mistake. He once told Mr.
Everard that he had just played ninety consecutive
holes without one stroke made otherwise than he
had intended. Judged by the standards of today,
in so far as these comparisons are ever worth
making, he lacked hitting power, but he must have
been a terrible man to beat. To James he represented no
doubt all that was great and heroic from the far-away
outside world of St. Andrews, and the boy followed
him round with adoring dog-like eyes; followed as
near as he could so that he might touch, if not the
hem of his garment, at any rate his bag of clubs,
hear some of the words of wisdom that fell from the
great man's lips and pass them on later to privileged
companions. That he would be able to retail any
such words as spoken to himself was more than he
dared to hope, and yet this wonderful thing happened.
The champion was a kindly man and was touched by

his youthful admirer; so when the game was over he made him play a shot or two. Then he made the boy play them again, that he might watch more precisely the way he did it. Finally he patted him on the shoulder, told him to play as much golf as possible and practise as hard as he could and he would be Open Champion some day. I wonder if James told that last remark to the other boys. I rather fancy he did not but hugged it to himself, gloating over it in strictest privacy and touching the stars with uplifted head.

Chapter II

From Slavery to Freedom, 1883-1893

WHETHER those treasured words of Jamie Anderson's were repeated by the boy to his father I do not know. If they were they fell upon deaf ears. Neither father nor mother could endure the notion of golf as a profession, and if we try to put ourselves in their places at that time we may think that they were very likely right. In Scotland with a few exceptions the professional golfer was little more than a superior caddie, making a rather precarious livelihood even if he were a good player, with too many idle and therefore tempting hours. He was a cheerful, feckless soul leading a hand to mouth existence with not much care for the morrow. Of course there were exceptions to this rule, not merely monuments of affectionately regarded respectability such as Tom Morris or Charlie Hunter, but others less well known, steady-going and prosperous men with a green to keep or a club-maker's shop. But the clubs that employed professionals were still very few. There would soon be many more of them, as the great golf tide began to surge in England, but its full force was hardly yet felt in 1883. Some Scottish professionals had already essayed the great adventure, crossed the border and done well, but there were destined to be far more of them towards the end of the 'eighties than at the beginning, and in any case the elder Braid, who was no golfer, would pay little attention to vague stories of an eldorado in England. So golf was definitely the forbidden thing. James must be apprenticed to a joiner. Moreover the joiner did not live in Elie or Earlsferry but in a little village three miles away. That meant a six-mile walk, for there were no buses in those days, a fact that cruelly cut down the few precious hours of daylight that could be given to golf. One feels for the young James as one does for the young Dickens thrust into the blacking business, with all his dreams of being a distinguished man growing fainter and more hopeless. Summer indeed was bearable, for there was generally time for a round in the long light northern evenings after the walk home, and all the year round there was Saturday afternoon. The summer Saturdays must have brought an exquisite agony of looking forward. Four years before he died James was travelling with his elder son from Elie to St. Andrews. As the train drew near Largo Ward, about five miles from Elie, he pointed to a row of cottages and told how one Saturday morning he had walked there to do some joinery work, then walked back and played fifty-four holes of golf.

When he was fifteen James joined the Earlsferry Thistle Club of which the *Golfing Annual* tells me that the entrance fee was two shillings and the subscription the same. He began to win competitions and to play regularly for the club team in matches against the famous and formidable St. Andrews Club, which a few years later could boast a side of twenty-five scratch players. At sixteen he was scratch himself, had won a scratch medal and broken the record of the course which now consisted of eleven holes. Enshrined in the pages of the first *Golfing Annual* stands the record 'Earlsferry Thistle Golf Club. Prize Winners in

1887: James Braid (two rounds of twenty-two holes) 93; James Keddie 94. Douglas Rolland when a member of this club on August 9th, 1884, did two rounds (eighteen holes) in 78, which is the record for the nine holes' round of the green.' James's winning score of five over fours stands comparison even with the mighty Rolland's, though to be sure I do not know whether those additional holes were short ones. I suspect they were, as the book tells me that on one part of the course there were sometimes three holes and sometimes five 'according as the course is laid out.'

Still hunting him through the *Golfing Annual* I find him in the following year winning the Burgh Medal, a Scratch Prize. Clearly by the time he was sixteen or seventeen the boy was a really good player, but he was much dissatisfied with his own game. He was, he says, an untrustworthy putter and that may well be, for in fact it was only by taking much thought that he made himself the fine putter that he ultimately became. But that which made him unhappy was his driving; he was a big strong boy who ought to have hit the ball a long way and he could not. He thought his swing was too short and managed gradually to lengthen it in the two years between fourteen and sixteen, but still that prayed-for length did not come. He was steady and straight but he was regularly out-driven by his contemporaries and had almost resigned himself to be a short driver for the whole term of a sad, frustrated life. And then suddenly his prayers were answered and he not only ceased to be a short driver but became and ever after remained a long one.

James's own account of this conversion is that he does not know how it happened. He declared, at any rate on paper, that it was a complete mystery to him, and the legend has long been established that James Braid went to bed one night a short driver and woke up next morning a long one. I am now, as the triumphant reporter so often observes, able to reveal the explanation. It has been given me by Ralph Smith who sturdily declares that it was no mystery at all, and I am bound to say that his explanation is at any rate a very likely one. Those who cultivate the mysterious and the sublime may cling to the supernatural. Here at any rate is Ralph Smith's more prosaic one.

James, he says, always played with very upright clubs, having the ball very near to him and having in consequence a markedly upright swing. The ball flew straight and high but came down to earth all too soon again. Ralph Smith was himself at this time serving his apprenticeship to George Forrester, a very well known club-maker at Elie, and among Forrester's customers was one Mr. John Berwick, a great fancier and buyer of clubs, and a very tall man of 6 feet 4 inches or so. One day he came to the shop and said he had a number of wooden clubs he wanted to get rid of: would Forrester send for them? Forrester accordingly did so and paid a shilling each for them. Smith instantly told James of this consignment of clubs, among which he was sure were some to suit him. James sped round to the shop as soon as he was free and found a number of drivers all with long shafts and heads much flatter in the lie than his own, so that he would have to stand farther from the ball. He picked one of them, went out to try a shot with it and behold, the ball flew far away into the distance. The club was thereupon bought for eighteenpence. George Forrester made a profit of sixpence and James in a state of bliss straightway outdrove all those who but lately had had the audacity to outdrive him. This is Ralph Smith's explanation and—perhaps it is my scientific blood—I incline to prefer it to that of a miracle. It is at any rate extraordinarily interesting.

It was some time after this event, miraculous or otherwise, that James set out on what must have seemed 'an awfully big adventure.' At nineteen he left home for the first time to go to work as a joiner at St. Andrews. Of all places in the world to which he might be sent this was surely the one he would have chosen, for here sooner or later would come the best golfers in the world and he could watch them all and might hope to play with some of them. And he did play with Andrew and Hugh Kirkaldy and other redoubtable players much to the benefit of his game. Such a course and such adversaries could not but pull him out. There was another great golfer there when James first arrived at St. Andrews, Sandy Herd, who was serving his last year's apprenticeship as a plasterer, but though they later became firm friends and partners in a famous foursome, it seems they did not then know each other well. Herd says in his autobiography: 'James Braid was working in St. Andrews in my plastering days, but as he was three years my junior and a backward young fellow with little to say, we did not pal up much then. Three years' difference in ages around twenty means more than three years around fifty.'

The Championship was played at Musselburgh in 1889 and at Prestwick in 1890. If it had been at St. Andrews in either year James might, greatly daring, have played in it, but he was short of practice and could not get nearly so much golf as he wanted. All is not gold that glisters; even at St. Andrews there are other things to do but play golf, and James's unfeeling employers insisted on sending him on jobs here and there about the country, so that he could not really settle down to his game. Generally speaking he had found that he could hold his own with the best of his playfellows except in putting; that was still a sore difficulty. How much this was due to his eyesight it is difficult to say. At some time when he was working as a joiner, the date is now lost, lime was accidentally thrown into his eyes, and he was never wholly free from its effects. Probably his eyes gave him more trouble as he grew older. His son Harry remembers him having to bathe them regularly night and morning, and his eyes were the only thing that ever, and that very rarely, made him take a day off from his work or his play, which were indeed synonymous. Undoubtedly these tiresome eyes did sometimes make putting, and especially the short putts, very difficult, but as later in life he became by hard work a very good putter indeed, they cannot have been wholly the cause of this early weakness.

In some ways St. Andrews had been a little disappointing; it had been hard to keep in form and in practice there; but in 1891 there was another move to Edinburgh and here he could get his golf regularly, on the Braid Hills, if not so much of it as he would have liked. As far as he had lost any of his early enthusiasm it soon came back. No doubt I ought to have seen the Braids but in fact I never have. I have always imagined it rather too mountainous for the best of golf, the sort of course that Andrew Kirkaldy would have described as suitable for a qualified goat. James however clearly held it in most grateful remembrance, for years later writing in *Great Golfers in the Making* he said: 'No turf like it, a course absolutely rich in sporting quality, greens that are magnificent and scenery from every point that is romantically beautiful, and air that makes one feel a good few years younger while playing.' And all that was to be had for twopence a round. No wonder there was a crowd. Golf had been making great strides in the last few years, not merely in England, and Scottish keenness was tremendous. 'When I went to my work at six in the morning,' he says, 'I constantly met many golfers coming back from the Braids after having had their early round; and on a Saturday afternoon I have gone up there to play at half-past one, and have had to wait until half-past five before being able to make a start, so great was the crowd waiting at the first tee.'

This does not sound the kind of golf for anybody of an impetuous temperament, but James was always a wonderfully patient man, as little inclined to any crisis of nerves as it is possible to imagine. Obviously he enjoyed the Braids and soon jumped back into his best form there. He joined the Edinburgh Thistle Club which had its club room at an hotel on Bruntsfield Links but played on the Braids. It was more expensive than the Thistle at Earlsferry, for the entrance fee was half a crown and the subscription eight shillings. James's handicap was plus two or plus three and he played for the club in those two well-known foursome tournaments which create great local patriotism and produce much fine golf, the *Dispatch* and the *Glasgow Evening Times* trophies. In one of his two years the Thistle lost in the final and in the other in the semi-final to the ultimate winners.

I go back for a moment to my researches in my green-coated *Golfing Annual*. In the volume for 1892-3 James Braid appears three times, twice as a player

and once as legislator. He was on the Council of
the Thistle Club, won the Gold Scratch Medal with
78 and also the Aggregate Scratch Medal. In the
following year he won the Gold Medal again, but
meanwhile he had done something more than that,
something that must always take a great deal of
doing: he won the Braid Hills tournament open to
all the Edinburgh and Leith Clubs. There was a
field of 140 players and he broke the record of the
course and naturally won the first prize. What this
score actually was, James with incurable modesty
does not say and my green book for once plays me
false. At any rate it represented the high water-
mark of James's career as an amateur, which in 1893
was destined to come to an end through his friend
Ralph Smith.

Smith had at that time ended his apprenticeship
with Forrester and was working at the Army and
Navy Stores, where he was or was at any rate on
point of becoming the man in charge of the club-
making. In the autumn of 1893 he had just come up
to Scotland for his holiday and was walking along
Princes Street when by pure chance he met his old
friend James. He thought him looking rather down-
cast. 'What are you making?' he asked him and
received the answer, '6d. an hour.' He could do
better for him than that, said Smith; how would
James like to come south with him, work at the
Stores as a club-maker and become a professional?
That was the one thing, said James, that he had
always longed to do. Very well, let him give notice
to his employers, come down to Elie and play some
golf and then at the end of Smith's holiday they
would go together to London. What James's parents
said I do not know. Probably they thought he was

now old enough to be master of his own fate. At any rate the two friends duly set out together to London where they lived together in various lodgings, at Sydenham amongst other places, and James began his career as a club-maker.

This was in itself something of an adventure for he had never made a club: but he was a craftsman, well accustomed to the use of wood and tools, and he knew a good club when he saw and felt it. There were some half a dozen club-makers in all besides Ralph Smith and none of them was aware that their new colleague had never made a club in his life nor did they find it out. The system was that each man should in turn work at one process, one to rough out the head, another to put in the lead and so on. The club would be passed along the line like a Ford Car in the Detroit Works. Thus James learned the different stages of his art and quickly became a master of it. He began by earning 8d. an hour and later rose to a shilling. He worked at the Stores from 1893 to 1895; and by that time he was Smith's right-hand man among an increased staff, and the Stores did a really considerable club-making business.

Mr. Henry Longhurst a little time since made some researches into the Stores catalogue of 1893 and the clubs proffered in it as made by 'experienced Scottish workmen.' I venture to borrow a few of his agreeable facts. If the names of the clubs provoke a smile their prices must produce the bitterest envy. There was the Bulger with its young family, the brassy bulger and the bulldog bulger: there was also the concentrated Lofter. Most of the clubs cost no more than 5s. 3d. though there were some very special clubs of 'extra-super' quality which cost 9s. The novice could almost buy the game of golf complete in a box, since for 36s. 9d. all told he could have four gents' clubs for 20s., a dozen balls for 10s., and a 'sling' for 6s. 9d. He could also, though this was not in James's department, get a deer-stalker cap for 2s. 3d. and for 30s. a golf suit with a Norfolk jacket. Those were emphatically the days.

The week-ends were now festivals of golf, for round London there was golf on Sunday which would have horrified Earlsferry and St. Andrews, or even Edinburgh. To Edinburgh indeed it was soon to penetrate, though under the rose; it was some eight years later that I remember driving out to Barnton for a Sunday game, with our clubs carefully concealed by the cabman beneath horse rugs. The two friends spent their Saturday afternoons and Sundays on various courses where the professional happened to be a friend of theirs—at Chingford, Sudbrook Park, Mid-Surrey and, above all, at Chiswick. I like to remember that, again a few years later, about the turn of the century, I used myself to play summer evening rounds on that charming little course, that has long since vanished under bricks and mortar. It had been a twelve-hole course when James first played there but there were nine holes when I knew it. It was delightful to rush away from an office, a little earlier than one ought perhaps, and catch a train from Waterloo. From Chiswick Station one had only to cross a road and open a gate in a wall and suddenly one was in a green spot that always seemed to me to have some magical quality about it. None of the nine holes was very long for there was not much room, so that there was just the suggestion of a cat's cradle about the course, but the turf was dry and the greens admirable; there were fine, stately trees, all the holes had some amusing quality, and the Short Water and the Long Water (especially the first of the two with its weeping tree by the edge of the green) seem in memory at least extraordinarily pretty. Nor was that all, for there was a lot of good golf played there by good young players, especially the Castles and the Finnises. The builder has in his time struck many a cruel blow, but none to my mind more brutal than that which deflowered dear little Chiswick.

The Editor of *Golf Illustrated* has most kindly allowed me to pursue James through his files, and there in the little old *Golf* in its scarlet jacket I found a reference to James and Chiswick. This was in a long account of the Chiswick Golf Club's Annual Smoking Concert in 1895 held in the Westminster Town Hall at which there were 400 people present. 'At the platform end of the hall was displayed an appropriate trophy of Golf Clubs designed by Mr. J. Braid of the Army and Navy Stores.' I cannot discover that Mr. J. Braid contributed to the programme but I find the names of several old friends, one of whom gave 'The Whistling Coon' amid great applause. All the songs and their singers are set out and there is an ecstatic description of 'the brilliantly lighted hall with its long row of green tables provided with all the paraphernalia indispensable to lovers of the weed.' What beautiful language people did use in those days just to describe ash trays, and how small a world was that of golf in which a whole column could be devoted to a smoking concert given by one suburban club!

I am however going too far ahead, for it was in December, 1893, not long after he had come to London, that James is recorded as playing his first professional match. This was on the most engaging little nine-hole course at Limpsfield where his cousin Douglas Rolland was then the professional. It was no doubt 'an act of friendliness on Rolland's part to contrive this match for the two young men from Earlsferry. Incidentally, I have been much struck in re-reading these old copies of *Golf* which I had first pored over as a schoolboy and then as an undergraduate, to find what a number of exhibition matches were being played in the early 'nineties. Today there is a professional circus that tours the country playing in an endless round of tournaments. Then there were hardly any tournaments beyond the Open Championship, but there were far more matches than there are today. *Golf* is full of them and the chief attraction, the man who played in most of them, was Rolland. A year or two afterwards, when Taylor had become the first English professional to win the Championship, he gave a great fillip to professional golf in the south and played in many such matches; but I believe that it was Rolland who largely started the fashion for them. With his tremendous hitting he must have been a magnet to the spectators and Ralph Smith tells me that he always received £20 for playing in a match. That was a big price for those days, and if he could regularly get it he was doing extraordinarily well. Light come, light go; whatever he got did not, we may be sure, stay long in his pocket. It was a little later that Rolland was to play a home and home match with Taylor over Winchester and Limpsfield. J. H. going to meet him at Winchester Station found Rolland, sure enough with three clubs tied with string, admitting that he felt extremely ill after some fearful spree in London on the way and demanding to be led to a chemist for a pick-me-up. Even the chemist could not prevent Rolland being some holes down at Winchester, but he duly got them back and more also at Limpsfield and won the match.

This first day's golf for James as a professional at Limpsfield consisted of two foursomes between Rolland and J. Pearson of Bournemouth on the one side and Charles Smith and James Braid of the Army and Navy Stores on the other. In the morning Rolland and his partner won by 2 and 1. In the afternoon Braid, we are told, holed a fine putt to win on the last green.

CHAPTER III

Nearing the Goal, 1894-1897

IN the next summer the Open Championship was to be played at Sandwich, the first time it had ever taken place on an English course, and James decided to enter. Just before the Championship there was an Open Tournament held at Stanmore and the prize list of £50 attracted forty professionals on their way to Sandwich, including nearly all the big guns except Rolland. It was said to be the largest professional tournament that had so far taken place south of the Tweed. The writer who described the play in *Golf* said that Stanmore could not fail to remind the visitor of Gullane. The comparison appears rather far-fetched but we may let it pass. James started last, paired with Albert Tingey of Brancaster and he created at any rate a mild surprise. Herd had done a 76 and was believed to be leading in the morning's play, but a tall young Scotsman, whom hardly anybody had ever heard of, equalled this score and instantly became in the words of *Golf* 'a personage of much interest.' The writer goes on to say that 'he fell off curiously' in the afternoon round, but in fact it was not curious at all on a first appearance in such company. He took 82 for the second round and so finished fifth, Cuthbert the local professional winning with 154, followed by Taylor, Tom Vardon and Hugh Kirkaldy in that order. James got £3 and an extra £1 as his share of the prize for the best individual round; there had been five 76's. It was by no means a bad beginning and he went hopefully to Sandwich.

There he started second, playing with Jack Burns the Open Champion of 1888, then at Wolverhampton. He did not begin by any means so cheerfully as at Stanmore for he took 91. To a large extent no doubt this threw him out of the hunt but it was not nearly so hopeless a score as the golfer of today would imagine. That modern golfer reading of Taylor's winning score of 326 can hardly believe his eyes, but I do not think anyone who did not play round Sandwich in its early days with a gutty ball can understand or even begin to understand how long and fierce it was. I saw it first a year later in the spring of 1895, and can confirm Taylor who says succinctly that it was 'a terror.' Given a wind many of the carries from the tee were undoubtedly too severe—even Edward Blackwell thought so—and the whole home-coming nine, relieved by but a single short hole, were, as the Duke of Wellington said at Waterloo, 'hard pounding.' Taylor's four rounds were 84, 80, 81, 81, of which the last might certainly have been lower but for one or two little accidents when on the threshold of victory. Whatever it may seem now, it was good enough then to beat all the best players in the world and beat them comfortably, for Rolland who was second was five strokes behind the winner. In short it must have been very good.

After his bad start James was steady enough with 84, 82, 84, but his 91 kept him out of the money. He finished tenth equal with Arnold Blyth, a very fine amateur golfer who played nearly all his golf at Sandwich, with Freddie Tait one stroke ahead of them. He had not of course done well enough to get a place in the professional side in the 'Gentlemen *v.*

Players' tournament which followed the Championship. There was much argument in *Golf* as to whether it should be a straightforward team match, reckoning the score by holes, or an American tournament, or, as it in fact was, a combination of team match and knockout tournament. The professionals as a whole proved undoubtedly the stronger side. Two of them, Taylor, the new Champion, and Rolland met in the final and Rolland won, but he had been lucky to beat Freddie Tait in the semi-final by the help of two opportune stymies.

We are not destined to hear much more of Rolland after that meeting. His splendid bolt was almost shot, rheumatism attacked him in the wrists and long before the coming of the rubber-cored ball he had become a purely historical figure. I should doubt if he ever tried to hit a Haskell in his life.

James had now begun to be known in the south but still only in a very small way. In *Golf* we find a 'Tee Shot' (one of the preliminary notes) announcing that J. Braid of Elie had recently broken the record of Northwood, 83, hitherto held by a well-known London amateur of those days, Franklin Ross. James had done 82 which certainly would have been much better but for a calamitous 8 at the hole with the deep, boarded bunker guarding the green, called Death or Glory, always the pride of Northwood. No doubt a good many London amateurs began to know him, but I fancy that to most golfers he was still very much of a nameless and partially mythical character. I was then an undergraduate in my first year at Cambridge and remember hearing of a wonderful player at the Stores who could hit the ball vast distances and was good enough to beat anybody, but his name, if I had ever heard it, did not dwell in my memory. Perhaps I preferred him as a romantic and mysterious unknown.

It was at the end of 1895 that James suddenly sprang into much wider fame, through a match which he played against Taylor, then Champion for the second year running, at West Drayton. To meet Taylor represented at once the highest ambition and the severest test of any aspiring professional. He was not only beyond question at the top of the tree by reason of his two successive Championships, but alike in achievement and in method of achieving he stood a little apart from all the other golfers. For one thing he was the first English professional to win the Open Championship; not the first Englishman, for that had been John Ball at Prestwick in 1890, but the first to break the almost exclusively Scottish ring of his professional brethren. For another he was generally thought to have set up a new standard of accuracy both in iron play and in the hitting of full shots up to the pin. In this respect also John Ball had to some extent anticipated him; the great amateur had shown what could be done in this matter of straight, long, fearless shots bang up to the flag; but the younger man had gone still further in this direction and he, as a professional playing here, there and everywhere, had been far more widely watched than the relatively unseen and retiring hero of Hoylake.

Moreover Taylor's style was in those days, *sui generis*, unlike the typical swing of the Scottish professional which we then naturally regarded as the only model. It was in this very year of the West Drayton match, 1895, that I first saw him when he came down to Worlington to play Jack White, and I with other Cambridge enthusiasts went over to look at him. Although I watched him so often afterwards and once or twice played with him, that first impression at Worlington remains something apart, extraordinarily distinct and vivid in my mind. Here was a man who seemed to play all his shots in much the same way and that rather like the way in which an ordinary mortal played a half-iron or even a mashie shot. It was not what we had been brought up to think of as a swing; it was a flick or a punch, delivered markedly firm-footed, with little obvious follow-through. It was impressive, fascinating, and in its straightness positively demoniacal. We now understood the aphorism that there were no hazards for him at Sandwich but the guide flags. He was not, I suppose, enormously long, but very few were going to gain anything perceptible on him in distance and the accuracy of his iron play was terrifying. If James could hold his own with such a man, in particular on a course where length was of no great value and there was much pitching to be done, then he would indeed have given his proofs.

James had had the advantage of playing a good deal at West Drayton and the members liked him so much that they got up this match, largely to bring him into public notice. West Drayton's place in golfing history has thereby been made secure, but the course itself has long vanished, even as has Chiswick. The traveller on the Great Western line soon after passing West Drayton Station may still see something that was once a built-up putting green and has long since lapsed into shapeless decay. As far as I know that is all that remains. It was a course of streamlets and willow trees and, it must be admitted, of unctuous winter mud. But London golfers had not such a choice of courses then; the star of sand and heather had not yet risen; West Drayton was easy to reach and was a friendly club. This match on the 20th December 1895 deserves some exactness of description because it had so important a bearing on James's future. I have read a long account in the files of *Golf* and have also had a good talk with Taylor about it. James himself from his prodigious memory could probably have recounted every shot and indeed he wrote that he remembered nothing more vividly in all his golfing life than the play in this match. The course was rather sticky and greasy after a frost and there was sometimes mud on the ball when on the green, mud that was not wiped off as it probably would be by the more lenient usage of today.

Taylor had never spoken to his opponent before; in fact he hardly knew him by sight, though he had heard the stories of the fine player at the Stores and knew he was good; but, as he said in a generous little speech after the match, he had not known quite how good; that had been a revelation to him. The course of the match was that Taylor was constantly getting a short lead to have it as constantly taken away again. Braid had the best of the driving sometimes by twenty yards; he was playing his chips and long putts well and actually holed one or two run-up shots from just off the green. Taylor was not getting his approach putts close enough but time and again was deadly from five or six feet, while Braid's short putting was not faultless.

Taylor went away at the start to be two up at the third and was soon pulled back; holed a fifteen-foot putt 'in grand style' to be one up and was again pulled back. Braid took a turn at leading with a two at the seventh and was two up at the eighth. Then the tide turned again and in the end Taylor coming with a rush was two up at lunch, both players having gone round in 73. The second round appears to have begun with a mild 'incident.' *Golf* thus describes it: 'Taylor had a fairly easy putt for the half, which he just missed, probably due more to the mud on the ball than his defective play. Thereupon someone in the crowd with conspicuous bad taste— we should hope he was not a golfer—loudly applauded the incident of Taylor having missed his putt, a piece of impertinence which Taylor very energetically and very justly resented. The incident however evidently irritated the champion during the next three holes and sensibly affected his play.'

That J. H. was energetic in his resentment I fully believe, nor, on my reading the passage to him, did he deny it. On the other hand it made him, if I know him, fight all the harder. Braid squared the match but Taylor always got his nose in front again; one up at the thirteenth and again at the fifteenth. The sands were nearly running out now and at the sixteenth Taylor had a chance of being dormy two but could not quite take it. The seventeenth was halved and he was dormy one. The eighteenth was a hole of a length that Braid could nearly drive, whereas Taylor was definitely short. He pitched safely to the green and was sure of his four. Braid played his run-up well but he was by no means dead. Exactly how long was the putt to save his neck? I do not know but it is described as a 'good' one. If one spectator had done James a good turn before, another nearly did him a bad one now. 'There is nothing,' he wrote years later, 'that happened in those early days of my professional career that I remember so well as an incident that occurred when I was making my last putt in that match, a putt on which everything depended, and which was in its way the most important putt that I had ever had to make in my life so far. I addressed myself to the ball twice and each time was just on the point of making the stroke when I was disturbed by a spectator immediately behind me striking a match. However, after two attempts he either got his pipe alight or decided to wait until the game was over, and at my third attempt to putt I got the ball away without interruption.' Down it went, the match was halved and a new planet had swum into the ken of golfers. A few years later when the Triumvirate were playing here, there and everywhere, the golfing public ceased, I think, to take any passionate interest in the results: sometimes one won and sometimes another. At the time of this West Drayton match, however, people were not yet blasé about mere 'exhibitions' and I can testify from my own youthful memory that it did make a real stir and James's win was regarded in the light of a noble piece of audacity.

I have kept to the end a little story told later in *The Beginnings of my Golf* by Mr. J. R. Gairdner, a fine Scottish golfer who then played much at Richmond and was referee in the match. Describing the last hole he says: 'I went to the flag and Braid, addressing the ball, suddenly stopped and said, "I'm not sure if I moved the ball or not." Seeing an old golfer, Mr. Buskin, standing close to Braid, I called to him for his decision, but before he could reply Taylor called out pleasantly, "Oh, never mind; play away, Jimmy." Mr. Buskin afterwards told me that Braid's ball had not moved.' Mr. Gairdner told the little story—J. H. does not recall it—to show the fine and chivalrous spirit in which the match was played on both sides. The two were destined to play many more later and the spirit remained unchanged.

Nothing would ultimately have kept James back but that match at West Drayton was the immediate making of him. When he played it he was assistant to his faithful friend, Ralph Smith, who had left the Stores and was professional at Hastings. By the following spring he had a job of his own at Romford in Essex where he remained for the next eight years. 'J. Braid (Walton Heath)' has long been familiar but 'J. Braid (Romford)' still sounds stirring in sufficiently elderly ears. Romford was, and I have no doubt is, a decidedly good course. It had not the beauties of sand and heather but in those days Woking was, I think, the only London course that had. It had some hedges and trees and, if I remember, a pond which may sound like a suburban mimicry of golf; but in fact it was by no manner of means bad golf, of an honest straightforward character with good turf, good greens and good length holes.

When James went there it was certainly one of the best of the London courses. I have always had agreeable memories of it from several close and pleasant matches there (I remember one against an old friend Willie Murray) and in particular because it was there that I first met James. I had actually set reverent eyes on him for the first time in the autumn of 1897 when I was at Penarth for the Welsh Championship meeting. There was to be an exhibition match between Taylor and Herd; at the last moment Taylor could not come and Braid was sent for and travelled through the night whereas Herd had been practising on the course the day before. On the morning of the match I saw James do what I never saw him do again; he took out a club, I think his trusty cleek, and hit several practice balls down the first fairway. I am not sure that he did not do another thing which I very rarely saw, namely run after them. At any rate he played a most impressive game and beat Herd rather severely.

It was, I think in the next winter, probably in the beginning of 1898, that my old friend H. G. B. Ellis, a very fine golfer with whom I had played much at Eton and who had played for Oxford when I played for Cambridge, took me down to Romford to match our best ball against Braid. To the best of my belief he won the first round and we won the second. I do not remember that he said much in the course of the match, being indeed, especially in his early days, a man of few words, but I perfectly recall what he said in his shop afterwards. He said that in the second round he had putted like a sweetie wife. So in fact he had, if sweetie wives putt badly as I presume they do, and that was the reason why we won. He putted with a cleek in those days, with a good deal of that 'knuckling' of the right knee which was so often to be found in the caddie-bred school of Scottish golfers. It is said to have been a heritage from Young Tommy Morris who was a very great putter indeed, but it was not a beneficial one; such tricks of genius seldom do much good to their imitators. Apart from that he was a desperate handful. He had looked formidably long at Penarth, but when one came personally up against him he seemed longer still. And in fact he was at that time probably the longest driver extant save for Edward Blackwell who was as a rule in California. Well might Horace Hutchinson talk of the 'divine fury' of his hitting. And when he went down, so to speak, to fetch the ball through the green with his brassy, with his right knee close to the ground, even as Rolland had been used to do, it was impossible to imagine the splendour of hard hitting

more gloriously portrayed. 'That old knee of his!'
as Bob Horsburgh in his shop said to me only the other
day. It was a terrific engine.

I don't think I ever played with James again at
Romford though I often did many years later at
Walton Heath, but I feel as if I had been a friend
of his from that day. Guy Ellis used often to play
with him there, sometimes with that beautiful golfer
his brother Humphrey as a partner, and James
remembered him well. Years later I was present
when somebody asked James who was the straightest
driver he had ever seen. He nodded to me saying,
'You know.' I thought I did and waited while other
members of the company made various suggestions—
J. H. Taylor, Bobby Jones and so on. At each the
sage shook his head and then gave the answer I had
expected—'Guy Ellis.'

However, I am going ahead a little too far and
must return to the beginning of 1896. James now
began to be in request for exhibition matches. The
days of the Triumvirate had not yet come. Taylor
was still unquestionably on the highest pinnacle,
though Harry Vardon's turn was soon coming.
James had not climbed quite to the heights yet,
but it was obvious that he must get there sooner or
later, very soon indeed if he could master the putting
art. I am not going as a rule to set forth his exhibition
matches which seem of no great interest today: but
at this the outset of his career they may be noted. He
beat H. C. Rawlins, an English professional, who was
the first Open Champion of America, by a pocketful
of holes, but had just the worst of two matches with
Taylor, one at Bristol and Clifton and the other at
Northwood, the Champion winning by 5 and 4 and
3 and 1 respectively. These last two matches were in

The finish of the drive.   James Braid on his 80th
birthday

April, the month that James settled down at Romford. It was on his own course at Romford that he gained his first success in score play. The club held an Open Professional Tournament in October of 1896 and James won handsomely in a strong field. He was first with 79 and 76; 155. Harry Vardon, who had by this time become Champion, was second with 78 and 80, 158. Herd and Jack White were next with 160 and Taylor 161. The scores no doubt seem high nowadays but Romford was no child's play, and I remember an amateur tournament there, with nearly all the best London amateurs taking part, when 80 was the best score for a single round. I must periodically remind my readers that these were gutty days, but I will not protest too much. The course seems to have pleased everybody for the account in *Golf* says that 'obviously Braid had been working at it late and early to get it into fine condition.' That is another little something that is worth remembering. The professional of those days had many other things to do besides play.

James had not played in the Championship of 1895 but he was of course determined to play in 1896 at Muirfield. He did what may be called respectably well finishing sixth with a total of 323 (83, 81, 79, 80) and gaining the not very generous sum of £5, but he was never really in the hunt as far as winning was concerned, and it is noteworthy that the long account in *The Golfing Annual* does not mention his name. It was a noteworthy Championship however for another member of the future Triumvirate, Harry Vardon. Taylor seemed likely to win the Championship for the third successive time and to equal the records of Jamie Anderson and Bob Ferguson and in a remoter past young Tom Morris. He was a tired man after three years of constantly having to uphold his position as Champion here, there and everywhere, but he very nearly did it. He was stopped by the man who, he is more and more firmly convinced as the years go by, was the greatest golfer he ever saw.

As it was in this year of 1896, soon after his victory, that I first saw Harry Vardon, I may here venture on a few words, even as I did in Taylor's case, as to my earliest impression of him. I had gone over to Ganton to play myself, and so did not watch him as I had Taylor at Worlington; I saw him play only a few shots, but the picture of those few remains wonderfully clear-cut. It is in one respect a puzzling picture because it is quite definitely different from that which is stored away in my mental gallery of golfers after watching him in later years.

The general opinion among golfers who saw Vardon after he had climbed to the highest point of his fame, is that his style was as nearly as might be the perfection of rhythmic beauty. I do not differ from it, as regards his later years, but that most certainly was not my original impression. To be sure his comparatively upright swing seemed then unorthodox in a way which it would not today. The typical Scottish professional's flatter and more sweeping swing was still, as I said a little while back, the generally accepted model. So it was natural to notice the suspicion of a lift in the taking up of the club and the narrowness, as it appeared, of the back swing. In fact there was I think more than a suspicion of a lift; it was extremely noticeable. I fancy also that his right elbow was not, as it was later, kept low and close to the side but went wandering away from his body. This is my belief from talking to Taylor and from reading what he wrote on the subject in his book.

'In his early days,' he says, 'Harry Vardon had a most ungainly style. A lift in his back-swing violated the principle of accepted orthodoxy. One expected to see, as a result, the ball swing away far to the right or sharply around to the left, but, as if in defiance of all accepted standards of what was right and proper, nothing of the sort happened. True, as the days went on, Vardon's lift became embodied into a style that was as graceful and perfect as any golf swing one is ever likely to see, which resulted in the perfect golfing machine.' That confirms my original feeling. 'Ungainly' is perhaps too strong a word, for there must always be a certain dignified and imposing quality about any style that is so immensely effective; but I think it is clear that Vardon's style did markedly change and that there was something to be said for Mr. Everard's view, when he and his brother Tom first appeared at St. Andrews: 'These Vardons are not pretty players.'

If this championship was a great triumph for Vardon it was one of the saddest of Sandy Herd's too frequent tragedies. He was a golfer full of courage, but one in whose ears the strains of 'See the Conquering Hero' were apt to sound too soon. He began with a tremendous 72, five strokes better than Taylor who was second. With the ball at his feet he lapsed to an 84 in the afternoon, and even so was second on the day only a stroke behind Taylor. Next morning he took the lead again with a 77 and then had a second and worse relapse with an 85. Meanwhile Vardon was steadily coming up from behind. On the first day he took 83 and 78, six strokes behind Taylor, and was quite unconsidered so far. On the last day he had a 78 and 77 against the holder's 81 and 80 and so caught him on the post. He won the

tie with 157 against 161. The new champion had, like
Braid, leaped into sudden fame through a match against
Taylor. A month or so before the championship Taylor
had gone to Ganton to play an exhibition match
against Vardon, who was reputed a good player but
had done nothing particular in any big event. He had
beaten the illustrious visitor by 8 and 7, and that was
a fact that we may be sure neither he nor Taylor had
forgotten when they came to play off the tie at Muirfield. Vardon's wholly invincible period had not
quite arrived yet, but he had taken the first great step
and was definitely ahead of James in the race for fame.

With the next year however at Hoylake it seemed
that James's turn had come, for he lost the Championship only by a single putt and with four holes to play
it was in his grasp or very nearly so. This was the
first time that the Open Championship had ever been
played at Hoylake and it was noteworthy for the
second victory of one of the two great Hoylake
amateurs, Harold Hilton. Hilton was now twenty-
eight years old and at his very best, with perhaps a
greater command of his wooden clubs than anybody
has had before or since, a masterly pitcher and with
unsurpassable knowledge of every twist and turn of
his native links. This Championship, looked at in
retrospect, seems from the beginning a duel between
him and James. They began with 80 apiece,
thoroughly respectable but no more. In the afternoon Hilton delighted his worshippers with a very
fine 75 only to find Braid doing better still, 74. Next
morning the situation seemed too much for both of
them. Hilton, without playing really ill, yet threw
away stroke after stroke by timidity near the hole and
finished in 84. James was not a great deal better
with 82 and there were several other people who

might win, in particular Pulford, a very good local professional, and Freddie Tait.

Hilton had the great advantage of an early start. So many Championships have proved the immense value of a man's 'getting his blow in fust' and setting a target for other men to aim at. Depressed over his morning round he determined on a good lunch ending with a large helping of trifle, which Mr. Smith, the famous steward, declared to be the best thing in the world on which to do a 75, the finest bit of prophecy, as it turned out, that ever was made. For a while the trifle worked like a charm. A 3 came at that most testing and alarming of all first holes, a 2 at the fourth, the Cop, and he had the first five holes in two under fours. Then he began to fritter away the strokes with four 5's running, including one at the short seventh, the Dowie, and 38 out was after such a start disappointing. However he had always said that to do a good score at Hoylake it was immensely important to start home 4, 3, 4, 3, for thus there was some reserve to draw on against the terrible cumulative length of the last five holes. That was just how he did start home and he made very few mistakes afterwards, though he did take a 5 at the Royal (the seventeenth) which was not then the formidable hole it is now. 75 was a great round and it was likely to win the Championship for him, but he had a weary and agonizing time of waiting; for Braid was setting out only a short while after he had finished.

Presently somebody came up to him and said, 'You must not mind too much if you don't win. That man Braid is a very fine player.' That was not particularly comforting and that man Braid after a poor start was doing uncomfortably well. The 5, 4, 6 was not cheering compared with Hilton's 3, 4, 5,

but then James in his turn had a 2 at the Cop and 40
in the circumstances was not at all bad. Then like
Hilton he started home 4, 3 and now he knew that
he wanted a 77 to win and 78 to tie. It was somewhere about this point that his rival came out for a
while to watch him and found the spectacle of James
just failing by a millimetre or so to hole his long putt
was more than he could bear. Still he was just
failing and he badly needed just one to go in. After
a great 4 at the Field (the fourteenth), and a 4 was
truly great there with a gutty, James could allow
himself 5, 5, 4, 4 to win, a by no means impossible
task; in fact the retrospective spectator may say that
he ought to have done it. A 5 at the Lake was good
enough; not so a 6 at the Dun where he went too
far with his third and got a bad lie beyond the green;
not so another 5 at the Royal; the putts would not drop.

So now Hilton waiting behind the home green could
at last feel tolerably at ease. James needed a 3 to tie
and that hole with a gutty was always a good 4. He
played two fine shots, his second with a cleek, and the
ball came on and on, almost over the hole to end some
ten yards or so past it. And now comes a curious
divergence between the two most accurate golfing
memories I have ever known. Hilton declared that
he did not feel frightened since the hole was cut in a most
difficult place with a swing away from it on either side;
that James's putt though perfectly struck duly swung and
passed to one side of the hole. James on the other hand
has written: 'I feel obliged to say that I did not consider
the putt by any means a difficult one, having due regard
to its length, and that I have the clearest impression that
the ball went not to the side of the hole, but right over
the very middle of it.' All we know is that the ball did
not go in and Hilton won by a stroke, 314 to 315.

CHAPTER IV

Breaking Through, 1898-1901

THERE were about this time more exhibition matches, particularly against Taylor. They had met with varying fortunes, Taylor having perhaps a little the best of it, but these matches were for the most part played on courses of no great merit and it would be monotonous to set out the results. Now Vardon had come prominently into the picture and we find James playing him at Halifax in 1897 and beating him, but again I do not propose as a rule to record any of their matches except for a particular reason. As James had so nearly won at Hoylake, 1898 ought to have been a good year for him but in fact his golf went back rather than forward. He himself has said in his book that he was not feeling very well that year. It was a rare state of things and a still rarer admission for him to make, for as I have said, save when his eyes troubled him he never took a day off, and as to his staying in bed such a thing was never heard of. The Championship was this year at Prestwick where Vardon, having gone back a little in 1897, began the victorious spell in which there was for two years or so no holding him, since he went up and down the country trampling down all opponents like some relentless Juggernaut. At Prestwick he only just won with 307, by a stroke from Willie Park, who was said, I know not whether correctly, to have been misinformed as to the score and to have believed that

his last putt was to win and not to tie. Moreover
should 'ifs and ans' ever be permissible then Harold
Hilton ought to have won that Championship, since
one stupid tee shot to the short Himalayas (he took
an unfamiliar iron in place of his trusty spoon) cost
him an 8 and even so he was but two shots behind
the winner. However, it was Vardon who did win
and he soon proceeded to show that he was beyond
all possible doubt the right champion. James came
ninth on the list with three poor rounds partially
redeemed with a 75 in the fourth.

If 1898 was a bad year for his golf it was a good
year in another way, for he was married on November
18th by the Rector of Upminster to Miss Minnie Alice
Wright of that parish. He was described as a 'golf
club-maker,' twenty-eight years old and his bride was
twenty-four. The faithful Ralph Smith was best man
and his name appears as one of the two witnesses.
The pair lived, if not then soon afterwards, at Golf
Lodge, Romford, and it was at Romford that their
two sons were born, James in 1899 and in 1901 Harry
Muirfield, whose name commemorates a great event
to which we shall come in due course.

Perhaps the moment when he has taken this step
in life is a suitable one to pause for a moment in the
narrative and look at the subject of it. But for some
inevitable change wrought by the years his face
looked then, I fancy, much as it did afterwards; it
changed comparatively little. On the other hand
there was a marked change in another way. Those
who only remember a somewhat portly and majestic
figure would be surprised to learn that such epithets
as 'lanky' used to be applied to him. He was a tall,
thin man, leggy like a colt. When I first saw him I
used to apply to him in my own mind John Nyren's

description of the man who thrashed the great Lumpy's bowling all over the field, 'a tall rawboned devil of a countryman.' He was 6 ft. 1½ in. in height and a few years later, according to the statistics in Mr. G. W. Beldam's book, he weighed 12 st. 6 lb., that is to say that for his height and his obvious strength he was not at all a heavy man. He said very little in those days, and indeed though he talked more towards the end of his life, he had always a considerable power of silence and, I fancy, disliked overmuch loquacity in other people. He was certainly, I should say at that time, a shy man. I remember at almost the turn of the century seeing a letter from him to a brother professional as to where they were to stay when they came to play at Aberdovey. James wrote that he did not want to be 'among the toffs.' Later in life at Walton he had a great deal to do with 'toffs' of various kinds and no man could deal with them better, but for that matter he always had a fine natural dignity and simplicity which made for no shade of difference in his demeanour, whatever his company.

I have had one very engaging ray of light cast on his life at Romford by Mr. Robert McKenzie, some-time Chairman of the P.G.A. and for many years, till he lately retired, professional at Stanmore. He was one of the first if not actually the first of James's assistants at Romford. They had met when James was playing in the north of Scotland and he had asked McKenzie if he would like to come to England. So the young Scotsman started off on this adventurous journey to an unknown country, feeling lost and anxious till he saw James waiting for him at Euston. It was a typically kind action. He took the boy to his house, found him rooms and generally looked after him. More than that, knowing that a boy fresh

from Scotland might be horrified by our un-sabbat-
ical behaviour in the south he said to him, 'We play
golf here on Sunday but you don't.' The boy was to
come to his house for dinner, tea and supper on that
day, a day to be kept for himself and in his own way.
No wonder that the highland boy became a most
faithful adorer who still thinks reverently of 'Mr.
Braid.'

As to the more technical aspects of James's golf his
putting weakness has already been hinted at. He
himself has written that he only overcame this by
hours of practice, but I really do not know when he
found time for those hours: I am pretty sure he
never putted in his bedroom like Ben Hogan, and I
know his old friend Taylor believes those virtuous
hours to have been largely mythical. Perhaps he put
them into his book to encourage his readers. Doubtless he thought hard about his putting and doubtless
also he gradually and greatly improved when he took
to the aluminium club, but beyond that I confess to
being a sceptic.

His swing was decidedly longer then than it was
when he grew older and its length in photographs
surprises me now, though I saw it often enough. Mr.
Beldam was taking his photographs for *Great Golfers,
Their Methods* in 1902 and 1903. That of Braid at
the top of the swing in a full drive shows the club well
past the horizontal, and so, though to a rather lesser
degree, does another of a full shot with an iron. A
few years later when the photographs for *Advanced
Golf* were taken, the swing had apparently shortened
a little but it was always an essentially full swing and
in his earlier days a most dashing one, with a very
free loose knee at the finish of the shot, when he really
went out for it.

On one small point I cannot be sure and probably never shall. Unquestionably James did not, like Taylor and Vardon, spontaneously discover for himself the overlapping grip and equally beyond question he adopted it, but exactly when did he make the change? I am convinced that when I first saw him in 1897 he did not overlap but had a more or less 'two V' grip, though with the left thumb down the shaft. This is confirmed by a large photograph in *Golf Illustrated* of March 1900. On the other hand Mr. Beldam's book as clearly shows the right little finger duly riding on the left forefinger. So somewhere between those two dates he made the change. I have a notion that on very cold winter days on Walton Heath when the club wanted a great deal of holding he reverted now and then to his youthful method.

As to his garments the reader may picture them much as he knew him in his later years. He never condescended to knickerbockers. Neither for that matter did Taylor, and though I think Herd once made the experiment, a concession to Vardonian fashion, he soon abandoned it. James always played in a coat, in later years no doubt in a waterproof jacket, but never, to the best of my belief, in a 'woolly' or 'jumper.' In fact nothing changed but the shape of his cap, as has the shape of all our caps. Gone for ever is the day of 'the little button on top.' I have always believed James to have been the introducer of mackintosh trousers. He was certainly the first man I ever saw wear them, when I accused him of having stolen them from a policeman; but that was later in Walton Heath days.

Now to get back to our chronicle year by year. Prestwick had been a disappointing year and Sandwich in 1899 was better but not really cheering. To be sure every one knew that humanly speaking Vardon must win and it was rather a question, as Walter Hagen used to put it, of 'Well, boys, who's going to be second?' His brassy play was at this time almost incredibly accurate besides being extremely long. It is no great exaggeration to say that he could put the ball as near the hole with his brassy as other people could with their short mashie shots. As there were in those days of the gutty a good many holes that he could reach with a drive and a brassy while almost everyone else needed a pitch as well, it will be seen what a hopeless business it was for most other people. In the spring of that year there was a professional competition at Mid-Surrey and in the qualifying rounds he had a 70 and a 74 and his total was eleven strokes better than the next man's. The professional of today goes racing round poor old Mid-Surrey in 67's and 66's but in those days there were a good many really long 2-shot holes to say nothing of two 3-shotters, and I still remember the consternation caused by Vardon's 70. It seemed to be a culminating achievement in face of which it was useless to struggle. He went on to beat Braid and Herd, and then poor Jack Rowe without much mercy in the final.

So with the Championship at Sandwich, a course which he loved and which exactly suited his long high carrying shots, no wonder the issue was regarded as certain. And win he did though not by such murderous margins as some of Taylor's. On the first day he only led Taylor by a stroke, 152 to 153, with Braid and Park next. He had been rather kind to his pursuers towards the end of the second round and let them come near to catching him. Next day—

a difficult windy day it was—he went away comfortably enough, again with some little relenting towards
the end, and won with 310, five strokes ahead of Jack
White, with Andrew Kirkaldy, Taylor and Braid
next in that order. Braid's story is really that of one
disastrous adventure and its consequences. In the
third round his ball hit the top of the Maiden; he
took 7 to the hole and was so shaken that he went on
6, 5, 6. His total was 85. Those who play the
Maiden today, a sufficiently commonplace iron shot
on to that lovely green, with bunkers certainly but
no very deadly ones, have no conception how formidable was the old hole with its full cleek shot (for Braid)
and full wooden-club shot as often as not for lesser
men. Right over the crest of that mighty sandhill,
with its black-boarded terraces, which frowns down
on the green, the ball must go and if it failed, liability
was almost unlimited.

Vardon was now cock of the walk in a way that
nobody has I think quite attained since. A few years
later James with his four championships in six years
was just as unquestionably the supreme player;
indeed that record was and still is unique, but it
was Vardon's feats that captured the popular imagination and brought flocking to the links a public that
had never been there before. 'Have you tried the
Vardon grip?' was a regular form of greeting, though
it was equally Taylor's grip, and Mr. Laidlay had
been using it for years before either of them. Soon
after this Championship, following the best part of a
year of haggling, came Vardon's match with Willie
Park who had rashly challenged him. The end was,
humanly speaking, certain, but Scotsmen are nothing
if not sanguine patriots, and a vast crowd came to
see the first thirty-six holes at North Berwick. By a

superb exhibition of putting Park clung close to the
champion and finished only two down, but at Ganton
he was annihilated. Finally towards the end of the
year Vardon went on his tour to America, travelling
victoriously up and down the country, leaving as he
himself thought a little of the finest edge of his game
behind him there and something perhaps of his fine
constitution as well.

Vardon duly came home to defend his Championship title at St. Andrews in 1900 and finished second,
but a long way behind Taylor who was in one of his
invincible and irresistible moods. Taylor and Braid
stayed together for the championship, as they did
many times afterwards. On this occasion lodgings
must have been hard to come by at St. Andrews, for
they shared not only one room but one bed. Each
night they duly rubbed each other down with em-
brocation, J. H. complaining that with that long
back of his companion's he had an unfairly large
share of the work to do. J. H. has never really liked
St. Andrews but he has played it magnificently,
winning two of his five championships there. I have
an impression that he set his teeth and determined he
would give St. Andrews a lesson. People had rashly
said it would not suit his pitching game and that he
could not run-up. Oh, wouldn't it and couldn't he?
He would show them and he did. He was first equal
with Vardon after one round and led him by four
strokes at the end of the day. He began the second
day by jumping the burn and getting his 4 to lead at
lunch by six strokes. And then he ran triumphantly
away with a 75—his 37 home was quite perfect—and
that was 309 and eight strokes ahead. It would be
absurd to say that anybody but Taylor could or
should have won that championship, and yet it was

one of the championships that James could least forget. Up to the hole he played magnificently, but his uncertain putting this time reached a climax of badness. There is no one whose estimate of his own game I would rather accept than James's, and this is what he wrote himself: 'That championship occasioned me more regrets than possibly any other in which I have taken part, for though at the end I was thirteen strokes behind Taylor, I consider that I have rarely had a better chance of winning or nearly, than I had that time if I could have putted in the least degree creditably. I was at the very top of my form, and I think that I was then driving better than I had ever driven before or have done since, and not only my driving but the rest of my game, except the putting, was as good as it has ever been. But my weakness on the greens was at its very worst at that meeting, and I was taking three putts over and over again, and no man can win a championship if he does that.' By all accounts James did not exaggerate his crimes in the least. He was putting for 3's and taking 5's. Mr. Everard wrote that his putting was enough to make angels weep and I have no doubt that in the kindness of their hearts they did.

It is darkest before the dawn and that long-drawn-out disaster on the St. Andrews greens was the prelude to James's first championship victory at Muirfield in 1901. Perhaps it may have had something to do with it by rubbing into him that he must, he really *must*, take a definite step about this putting. At any rate he took to the aluminium club which was in his hands, comparatively speaking, a magic wand, and from now on he became a very good putter with a slow smooth stroke which was a model of its kind. He was never, I think, proof against the short ones of which he could not entirely overcome his fear; he was never quite happy even when he was dead, but he became a fine approach putter; the way in which a few years later he would roll up the long putts stock, stone dead on those keen greens at Walton Heath will be remembered by all who played there with him. But I think his great strength on the green was as a middle-distance putter. 'I have yet to meet,' writes J. H. Taylor, 'the player who could hole the ten-yard putts with greater regularity.' It may be that 'regularity' is rather a strong word at that range, but undoubtedly James did during his best years, to which we are now coming, hole day in and day out what must have seemed to his adversaries a brutally large number of those middle-distance putts.

He had been playing well from the beginning of this year that was destined to end the lean years. On the way to Muirfield he left everyone else far behind with four rounds of 36, 34, 35 and 35 at Musselburgh. This was a really wonderful score, such as had never been done there before. The year before on the way to St. Andrews he had won at Musselburgh with 151 for four rounds of the nine holes, good evidence if any be needed, how altogether outstanding was his 140. This was done in a qualifying competition and he then went on to win the match play as well, beating Sandy Herd in the final. The days of that once famous course's glory are over now. Any one who loves the past will slow down his car on the way from Edinburgh to Gullane to look at the glory that was once Musselburgh, the home of the Parks and the Dunns, of Bob Ferguson and many another good golfer. He can see Mrs. Forman's and make a guess at Pandy and can well believe that this, for all that today it looks rather cramped and rough and derelict, was yet once a

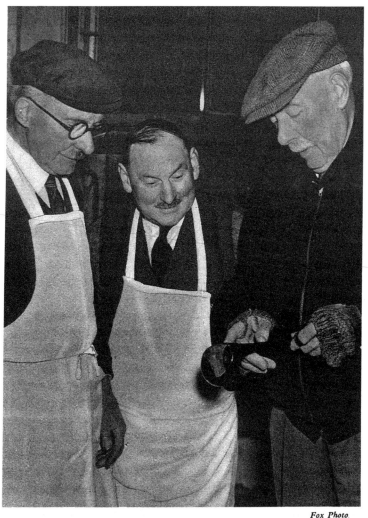

Fox Photo.

James Braid in the Club House at Walton Heath on his 80th birthday with (left) W. Brown, 41 years at the Club and (centre) Robert Horseburgh, 37 years at the Club.

worthy test of heroes. 'I shall never regret,' wrote
Mr. J. E. Laidlay, 'having learnt my golf on the fine
old course at Musselburgh, as it was in those days, for
it was a splendid course. . . . I have always thought
and still think that anyone who had learnt to play well
on Musselburgh could give a good account of himself
on any other golf course in the world.' The course
had received its real death blow when the Honourable
Company had taken the championship from Musselburgh to their own private course at Muirfield in
1892, but it had been the scene of the first half of a
big match between Willie Park and Taylor in 1897.
In 1901 the rubber-cored ball had not yet come to
kill it once and for all; it was still, and that rightly, a
course of consideration, and a score of four under an
average of fours there was truly notable. Willie Park
had won the last Championship played there with
155.

James's start at Muirfield was far from cheering
for he hooked his tee shot out of bounds into the wood
at the first hole and took 5 instead of the orthodox 3.
He went on making mistakes and dropping shots till
he had taken 43 to the turn; then he put away childish
things and came home splendidly in 36. This kept
him at least in a comfortable position. For some
time Taylor, Willie Park and Kinnell led with 78;
then Vardon ousted them with 77 and that was the
leading score. In the afternoon Park went all to
pieces with 87 and Taylor fell away badly with 83.
Vardon was very steady as in the morning, with 78
and a total of 155. James again made a rather de-
pressing start with 4, 6, 4, 5—four strokes dropped in
four holes. After that he was at his best, turned in
40, which was good enough in the circumstances, and
again came home in 36, to share the lead with Vardon.

In the crucial third round Vardon and Taylor
were drawn to play together, to fight over again their
battle of 1897, a very doubtful advantage to either of
them. James went out later and so knew what they
had done and what he probably had to do. Vardon
was the man for him to watch for Taylor was seven
strokes behind both of them and the rest of the
world had dropped strangely far astern. It was a
case of the Triumvirate, not yet so called, first, and
the rest nowhere. By lunch time the position had
been made much clearer; it was now James's
Championship, though perhaps he did not let himself
think so. Vardon had thrown strokes away and had
taken 79; Taylor had come with a fine rush and a
74 to be within two shots of him, but that was of little
comfort since Braid had had a 74 too.

This 74 of James's was, I gather from Mr. Everard's
account in *Golf Illustrated*, made or rather perhaps
saved from being marred by three consecutive and
crucial holes on the way home. He was the only man
who could reach the twelfth hole—this was the old
Muirfield, remember—with an iron for his second but
he missed a putt and took 5. At the thirteenth he had
to play a horrid shot over woodwork in a bunker, as
it is described. I can visualize it well and the sloping
green on which the ball had to be pitched. The ball
duly overran the green and James holed a five-yard
putt for his 4. At the short hole over the cross-bunker
he holed another good putt for his 3 and yet another
nasty missable one for the par 4 at the fifteenth, the
hole where it was all too easy to be short in the second
and also so fatally easy to be too strong and in the
bunker behind the green. So there were three strokes
saved which made all the difference in the world.

The last round went well to begin with but, as it

progressed, anxiety told its natural story of timid putting and the strokes dropped here and there. Moreover the too enthusiastic spectators slapped him on the back and told him repeatedly that he was sure to win. I mean actual physical slapping on the back such as made him positively sore and stiff by the time the round was over. To be sure the Scots are eminently patriotic and no Scot had won since Willie Auchterlonie in 1893. Even so the imbecility of spectators, who have the best intentions, is and will always be incredible. James was growing just a wee bit apprehensive but he steadied himself to finish in 80 and that was more than good enough. Vardon had crept up on him but only to the extent of two strokes and Taylor was one behind Vardon. James won by four shots with 308. He had done it at last.

For those who were awaiting him behind the home green there was one unpleasantly dramatic moment. As he played his second with his cleek, something bright and shiny was seen to travel a few yards along the ground. An instant later came the reassuring thud of the ball on the green. He had broken his cleek in playing the shot and a hunter of souvenirs resolutely refused to surrender the head.

No victory could have been more popular whether in England or Scotland, both on account of the winner's many lovable qualities and because it was so universally felt that he had earned it; it was his turn. Mr. Everard hastened to make amends for his remarks about his putting of a year before. Then he had described James as 'as bad as Old Tom at his worst.' Now he 'might be described as a good holer out on the average.' He had moreover, and here I respectfully agree from my own memory, 'abandoned the mischievous habit of knuckling over' and kept his body quite steady. Another critic, that rather complacent old party, the Rev. Gordon McPherson, D.D., in his day one of the very best of the amateurs, took some of the credit of James's improvement to himself. 'Braid scolded me,' the doctor wrote, 'for having said on former occasions that he would have been champion if he could only putt. I advised him to use a wooden putter for long putts and a cleek for short ones and he took my advice at Musselburgh.' Nobody need grudge the Doctor his harmless little crow, but I am very sure of one thing, that the putter was not of wood, but the aluminium club that was for so many years to be a faithful ally.

CHAPTER V

The Coming of the Haskell, 1902-1904

JAMES had come into his kingdom and he, Vardon
and Taylor travelled up and down the country,
to Hayling Island, Cromer, Sheringham and, indeed,
where not. In October they played with the local
professional, Charles, at Totteridge, which a year or
so later was to become Vardon's home course for the
rest of his life. In the report of the play—Taylor
first, Braid second, Vardon third and Charles out of
the hunt—the three are, as far as my researches go,
called for the first time 'The Triumvirate.' There is
only one of these games that particularly interests me,
though James was in fact beaten in it, and that is both
on account of the battlefield and the obviously fine
play. This was a match between Braid and Taylor
on historic Blackheath. Taylor won by 5 and 3,
holing the three rounds of seven holes in 33, 33 and
30, beating the record both for one round and for
three. I knew Blackheath fairly well at one time,
having had some severe experiences there of Mr. F. S.
Ireland, a strong golfer on any course but a much
better one at Blackheath than anywhere else. His
best scores, and he had won many, many medals
there, were respectively 31 and 99. J. H. and Vardon
had both equalled this score and now J. H. gained
for himself one of the records that is safe for ever, for
alas! golf on Blackheath is no more. 105, an average
of 5 a hole, used to be deemed, and rightly, a very

good score on that flinty heath with its two enormously long holes, its cruel lies and its intersecting roads with precipitous edges. For all its roughness there was something great about that golf on the heath, something that put it in an altogether different class from the ordinary suburban park. The greens moreover, for all that the whole world could walk over them, were good enough and had the archaic charm of having no tins in the holes. I cannot imagine any course on which I should have so little liked to face either of those two great men, and very few on which I would rather have watched them. Yes, Blackheath 'had something,' as people say nowadays. J. H. tells me he did play very well indeed for that 96 and I am very sure he did, the more so as it would to my mind have been James's course to a nicety. 'It is,' he says in his book, 'an achievement that gives me more than a passing thrill.' Blackheath no doubt became far easier with a rubber-core, if only because of those lies out of which the gutty wanted so much forcing. I do not think however that that record was ever beaten and in any case Blackheath was a gutty course and its red-coated veterans were gutty golfers. With the Haskell's coming its sun had set.

One more competition in 1901 deserves mention not so much for its own sake as for what it portended. This was the first meeting, on the old Tooting Bec course, long since vanished, of the London and Counties Professional Golfers' Association. It represented the first application of the trade union principle to the golfing profession. There are points about trade unionism that a good many people do not like, but I have no intention of indulging in a political discourse, of which indeed I am quite incapable. Enough that the golf professionals learned that they could accomplish more for their own benefit when they were united than as separate individuals. It is truly surprising now to think that it is only in comparatively recent times that the professionals have been able to come into the club-house at an Open Championship meeting, and that represents only one of many respects in which their treatment has grown more civilized and their station has been immeasurably improved. That is not all due to the fact of the professionals having their own body to represent them, for the position of all professional game-players has greatly and properly altered during the present century; but the movement of which this London and Counties Association was the beginning, has had at least something to do with it.

It was originally founded, I believe, because there was a tendency among some clubs to let the shop and its opportunities to the highest bidder. Thus the professional would lose the main attraction of his business, the one steady source of income on which he ought to be able to rely. So obvious an injustice led to a general agitation that was quickly successful and this success naturally led to the formation of the Association. Taylor was the first Chairman, an office he held for years, and James was the first Captain. Appropriately enough the Chairman won at Tooting. This London and Counties Association soon took in more and more sections from other parts of Britain and became the Professional Golfers' Association, as we have now long known it. No one can doubt that it has done a great deal in various ways to improve the status of the professional golfer and its benevolent fund has done much good among its members. Now and then it has suffered the unpopularity that attaches at times to all trade unions, but this is not the place to discuss questions of the 'closed shop.' That its general influence has been for the good of professional golf cannot, I think, be doubted by any reasonable person, neither can anybody doubt that if J. H. was the vital spark without which the Association might never have been, James was always a wise and valuable counsellor. He was Captain of it in all five times as Open Champion and in 1946 when the American, Sam Snead, won the Championship and could not hold the office, it was conferred on James again. He was a man very far from prompt in committing himself, and the inclination of his mind was against rather than for any new step. He would sit silent for a long time during a meeting but when he did say something it was eminently sensible and worth listening to and could have on occasions a decided tang, a most characteristic flavour of its own. He was a member both of the Executive Committee and the Benevolent Committee up to the day of his death.

If the end of 1901 saw the beginning of a movement very important to professional golfers, 1902 saw something approaching a revolution to affect the whole world of golf. This was the coming of the first rubber-core ball, the Haskell. The story is now almost as dim as that of the coming of the gutty and the departure of the poor feathery in 1848. So perhaps it may be briefly told. The first British golfer to play a shot with the ball was almost certainly J. H. Taylor when he was in the United States in 1900. He arrived at the Wheaton course, near Chicago, the scene of the Open Championship, in which Vardon was his chief rival, to find a parcel from an unknown Dr. Haskell, containing some balls of a new type, with a request that he would try them. He had a shot or two but did not for the moment fully appreciate the ball's power, perhaps because he had already made up his mind that it would be dangerous to make so drastic a change on the eve of the Championship. So he stuck to the gutty and Vardon beat him by two strokes. Soon after he gave the Haskell a longer trial and realizing what it could do, came to the conclusion that the gutty was doomed; but he did not for the present adopt the new ball.

That was in 1900 and in 1901 a certain number of Haskells came gradually filtering into this country, but I think very few people had yet heard of them; at any rate no whisper of them had reached me. Horace Hutchinson knew of them because a brother-in-law had brought two dozen home from America and then, growing disgusted with them, had handed them over to Horace. He was a convert rather uneasy in his conscience, being at the time interested in a new solid ball made of material called Maponite; but he went so far as to induce his partner in the Biarritz and Pau foursome to use the Haskell and they duly won the match. Still it was unknown to the mass of golfers and remained so till it suddenly burst on the world at the Amateur Championship at Hoylake in May of 1902.

I have, I know, told before how I first heard of it, but I may be allowed to do so again because the otherwise dull and egotistical little story shows how brief was the warning that most people had had of the revolution. At Euston where I was catching my train to Liverpool, I met a golfing friend from Lancashire just arrived in London, the late 'Sandy' Hogg, who asked me if I was going to play in the first match between England and Scotland immediately before the Championship. I said I had hopes of doing so, whereon he asked whether I meant to play with a

Haskell. I said 'What is it?' He said I should make a great mistake if I did not use it and we parted. When I got to Hoylake sure enough a certain number of people had got some of the new balls but no more were to be had for love or money and I gave up the attempt in despair.

The Haskell was used by both the winner Charles Hutchings and the runner-up, Sidney Fry, and from that moment was clearly destined to be the ball of the future, unless some firm step was taken to repel the invader and establish the solid ball by law. I think that most people who are old enough to have played the game with the gutty would agree that a certain insistent demand for accuracy of hitting and for power of control in the wind went out of golf with the gutty, to its detriment alike as a game of skill and strength. But do any of them think that any legislation could have prevented the use of a ball that made golf perceptibly pleasanter, easier and more flattering to the general run of golfers? I do not believe that it could. I am full of admiration for John Low, Mure Fergusson and others who fought the good fight for the solid ball, but I think they were fighting a hopelessly losing battle. Anyone who cares to read anything of what has long since become a purely historical controversy will find the arguments against the rubber-core set out by John Low, its most eloquent and persistent adversary, in his chapter in *The Royal and Ancient Game of Golf*. He wrote that chapter in 1910, when, looking backwards, he was still convinced that he had been right. His view was that in the beginning 'all that was necessary was that a ball containing a core should not be allowed, as it was plainly too easily driven to suit the balance of the game.' I cannot myself believe that any such law would have stopped the new ball, but today the point is an academic one.

In that summer of 1902 all the great ones of the golfing earth were canvassed for their opinions of the new ball and all the lesser ones were trying by hook or by crook to buy one. The professionals almost to a man expressed themselves against it, partly, I have no doubt, from conviction but partly also perhaps from those business motives which had originally set Allan Robertson against the invading gutty. *Golf Illustrated* was full of letters on the topic of the hour. Taylor, speaking from his experience of the ball in America, took up his testimony against it declaring that the gutty was in imminent peril. Vardon, too, held that it would lessen the skill of the game, and these two never wavered afterwards in their opinion. Sandy Herd, who was destined to win the Open Championship, and that his only one, with a Haskell, succinctly expressed the hope that everybody would use it except himself. Braid declared that the Haskell did not carry further than the gutty though it could run further, and that on the green he had found it apt to jump out of the hole; further, his economical soul was vexed by its tendency to split.

The Open was that year at Hoylake, as the Amateur had been (no one course is ever so burdened today), and the great majority of the professionals kept their vow and played with the gutty. The one wise renegade was Sandy Herd, who was converted in a practice round he played with John Ball. John lent him a Haskell with which to play a shot or two and his mind was instantly made up; he would eat his words and use it. At the end of the first day Vardon led with a magnificent 72, a really great score at Hoylake with a gutty, and a 77. Next, four strokes behind, came

Ray and Herd at 153, the latter not altogether satisfied with his Haskell but hoping for better things
from it next day. One stroke behind them again
came Braid with 154.

Sure enough next morning Herd's Haskell really
began to show what it could do. There was a difficult
wind but he was round in 73, seven strokes better than
Vardon who had taken 80. So had Braid and his
hold on the Championship seemed hopelessly gone.
With a round to go the scores were Herd 226, Vardon
229, Braid and Taylor (who had pulled himself up
with a 77) 234. Herd played one of his too familiar
over-anxious last rounds; he had tragedies at the
Punchbowl and the Alps and was so determined to
be over the cross-bunker at the last hole that he
came near to wedging his ball under the fence beyond
the green. He had left Vardon every chance of
catching him and caught he nearly was, for Vardon
wanted a 4 to tie going to the eighteenth. He jumped
the cross-bunker, but left himself a six-foot putt to
hole and missed it. Herd could now, as it seemed,
breathe freely. Certainly he must have thought that
all fear from Braid was over, if he knew that the
reigning Champion had started 6, 4, 5, 4—three
strokes gone already. After that James did well
enough to be out in 40, but even so he had eight strokes
to make up on the leader with only nine to play.
And yet he, oh! so nearly did it. 4, 3, 4, 3, 4, 4, 4
left him with a 3 and a 4 to tie and in his putt for the
3 at the seventeenth the ball jumped right over the
middle of the hole. So, as in Hilton's year, he was left
to get a 3 at the last hole and once again the task
proved too much, but there have been few more
gallant forlorn hopes than that 34 home. It suggests
Frank Stranahan's great home-coming on the same

course in 1947 when he wanted a 2 to tie with Daly and came within about two inches of getting it.

Herd's victory sealed the doom of the gutty past all doubt. It is a truly remarkable fact that the very full account in the number of *Golf Illustrated* following the Championship makes no mention of the fact that Herd alone of the leading professionals had used the Haskell. Certainly everybody who knew anything about golf knew it perfectly well. I can only think that the then Editor, who had the sternest views on the subject, did not wish to encourage his readers to believe in this new and outrageous ball. Later in the same year in September, referring to the number of records that had been broken during the summer, he wrote: 'Herd is, as far as I know, the only one who plays with the new ball, but he is not the only record-breaker.' It made little difference what he or any-one else said, for rightly or wrongly, the man in the street was determined to have a ball which helped him, as he believed, to bridge something of the gulf that divided him from the best players.

Apart from his original letter I do not think James made any great protest against it. It was the ball people wanted and it was his business to let them have it and to learn to play with it himself as well as possible. He assuredly mastered it, for, except for his first Championship at Muirfield, he won all his greatest victories with it. And yet he always struck one as essentially a gutty player. When some years after-wards four of the leading professionals, he, Vardon, Taylor and Duncan, played in a competition with gutty balls he was the outstanding figure and his power with it was crushing in its magnificence. The Triumvirate's matches were now enlarged to include the new champion, Herd, as a fourth member, and

Arthur Croome suggested that they should be called, in the language of piquet, the 'Quarte Major.' In this year, too, James did—I will not say his first job as a golfing architect, but the first of which I have found any record. He advised as to the altering of the course at Pyecombe in Sussex and *Golf Illustrated* announced, almost superfluously, that he 'thought highly' of it.

1903, which was to be his last year at Romford, was a rather disappointing one for James as far as the Championship was concerned. It was played at Prestwick and before the Championship came the first professional international match in which he beat Vardon by five up and four to play and Scotland won by nine matches to eight. Scotland incidentally were never destined to win again. They twice halved the match, but otherwise suffered an unbroken line of defeats. James had begun well at Prestwick, but after that it was Vardon's Championship all the way. He thought it the best of his wins and so it assuredly was considering that he was quite unfit to play. It was not long afterwards that his health really broke down and he had to go to the Sanatorium at Mundesley. He felt ill during all four rounds and during the last was so faint that he was afraid he would not be able to finish. And yet he won easily. His morning rounds were magnificent, 72 and 73, and in the afternoons when he was tiring fast he kept steady with 77 and 78. To show Vardon's powers and also the recklessness of his unconquerable courage, he went to Western Gailes on the very next day after the Championship to play in a tournament, broke the record with a 68, and won comfortably.

James was never really in the hunt in this championship, putting, as he says, timidly all the time and ending fifth, ten strokes behind Vardon. He had begun to think that Prestwick was a fatal course for him, an impression of which he was to be thoroughly disabused in 1908. If he had, comparatively speaking, failed in the Championship he had compensation in winning the first *News of the World* tournament which was from the beginning virtually the professional match play championship and has since been officially recognized as such. The first prize was £100, with ten others to match (they have been considerably increased since then) and from the start this tournament caught the popular imagination. It was a change from the exhibition matches of which people were growing a little tired, just as today they are growing tired of the endless round of seventy-two-holes tournaments in which the professional circus takes part. The play in the exhibitions was always good and strenuous, but it did not perhaps so very greatly matter which of the big men won. In this tournament it did obviously matter and, besides, the big men were apt to be hunted hard, possibly even hunted to death by the little ones. In an eighteen-hole match, as the Amateur Championship has so often shown, David has a great chance of frightening Goliath and may beat him. It is noteworthy that not till the fifth year of the tournament when Braid beat Taylor at Sunningdale did two of the Triumvirate meet in the final.

It was played at Sunningdale in 1903 and the big guns were all there except poor Vardon, who was in his Norfolk retreat, forbidden alike to play golf or to smoke his pipe. James began comfortably by beating Jack Ross by 6 and 5 and went on to beat Hepburn, a good golfer who went later to America, by 5 and 4. In the third round he met A. H. Toogood, originally from Bembridge in the Isle of Wight, a golfer of really great possibilities. He never quite lived up to them, though to be sure he reached the final of this tournament the very next year. He gave James a considerable fright by some desperate putting on the way home. James was one up at the eleventh and then Toogood began. He squared at the thirteenth with a long putt and went on holing putts till he took the lead at the sixteenth. James came back at him with a three at the seventeenth and the last hole was halved. At the nineteenth Toogood having had his ration of long putts missed a very short one for the half and Goliath was safely through.

James beat Taylor with as much comfort as he could possibly expect, for he won by 3 and 2, and now had to meet Ray in the thirty-six-hole final. It was a fine match and if James's victory did not wholly depend on a single shot, he owed that shot a good deal. He was a hole or two up at the turn in the second round and from the high tee at the tenth, with its exhilarating view, he drew his tee shot into the bunker that lies on the left of the fairway. The reverent pilgrim may go and stand in that bunker and 'musing there an hour alone,' like Byron at Marathon, consider his chances of reaching the green in the dim distance. Ray was on the course and would, humanly speaking, get a four. The ball lay well enough in the bunker but there was a pretty steep bank and nothing but a fairly straight-faced iron could possibly reach the green. James took the risk and his big iron, duly reached the green and then, adding insult to injury, he holed his putt for 3, his ball touching Ray's as it passed, so nearly had he been stymied. After that no wonder he won by 4 and 3.

That tournament was, I think, the last to be won by

James Braid (Romford) for in April of 1904 he had come to Walton Heath. Here he was to live, in his house dutifully called Earlsferry, for the rest of his life and to make of the place something of a shrine for all golfers. Walton Heath is and always will be one of the great inland courses, big, fierce and exacting, blown upon by mighty winds, and having to my mind some indefinably seaside quality in the problems which it sets the golfer. It has far more competitors now than it had in 1902 when Mr. Herbert Fowler began to survey that big stretch of golfing country. Woking was some ten years older and Sunningdale had come into being with the new century; there were other heathery courses near London such as charming little New Zealand. Scattered about the country too it is possible to think of Aldeburgh and Woodbridge and above all Worlington in Suffolk, Woodhall Spa in Lincolnshire and Ganton in Yorkshire, but the inland courses of sand and heather and fir trees were still comparative rarities: the London golfer played mostly on mud unless he could dash away to Sandwich or Deal, Rye or Littlestone for the week-end, and a heather course which was opened under prosperous auspices, where things would clearly be done on a big scale, was a decided event.

It was a vast, wild stretch of virgin heath when Mr. Fowler first began to prowl over it on behalf of his brother-in-law, Mr. Cosmo Bonsor, and others who were interested, and gradually to evolve in his 'immense and brooding spirit' the ideal spots for his greens. The heather was then between two and three feet high over the whole of that great tract. It was the sort of lonely, desolate waste that fierce old Cobbett, who loved only cultivated fields, would have

called 'as vile a spot as ever I saw in my life.' But it
was a spot to bring joy to the heart of one who like
Mr. Fowler had made a study of golf architecture
and always longed for an opportunity to lay out a
course. It was in August 1902 that he began his
survey. Herbert Fowler was rather a 'harbitrary
gent' and did not suffer other people's ideas very
gladly, but he loved his work and had imagination
and a good 'eye for country.' I never knew anyone
who could more swiftly take in the possibilities of a
piece of ground, and I think his clients sometimes
thought, quite unjustly, that he had not taken sufficient
pains, because he could see so clearly and work so
fast. Now over this task at Walton he had taken the
best part of two years. It must have been a desperate
problem to know where to begin on that huge expanse.
By his own account he first decided on the fascinating
green which became that of the sixth hole and worked
backwards from that. He produced something on a
rather grander and more severe scale than had yet
been seen inland, and at least two of the holes, the
sixth, then a short hole, and the really noble seventeenth, today the sixteenth, soon became famous. The
course is probably longer now than it was then, for
I am told by those who know every inch of it that the
ground was faster in its early days and that James
could and did hit drives to places that no mortal
could reach now. Be that as it may, it was uncommonly long when it was opened, judged by the
standards of those days, and was what it still is in a
unique degree, essentially 'big' golf away from the
sea.

It was in August 1902, as I said, that Mr. Fowler
had begun his survey. In April 1904 James moved
to Walton from Romford and in May the course was

opened with a due flourish of trumpets and a special train to Tadworth to convey all the notabilities who came to see the course and the play. This was a three-ball match between the Triumvirate, Vardon now having made so good a recovery that he beat Taylor by six holes and Braid by three. The best approximate score of the day was Vardon's 76, and it must have been a very fine score indeed on the new fairways and greens with the heather still untrampled and un-hacked by the niblick. Later in the year at the beginning of July I find it recorded that James had holed the course in 70.

It must have been a decided advantage to James to have such a training ground. To be sure his game needed no pulling out; he could grow no longer as for instance Sherlock did when he left Oxford for the greater spaces and more exacting holes of Stoke Poges. But for a man, no matter how fine a golfer he is, it must be a help to be playing constantly on a course of really high class. Moreover, the big keen greens with plenty of borrows in them must have been good for his putting, none the less because they were often blown upon by winds of seaside vehemence, and in fact his approach putting on the Walton Heath greens was lethal in its accuracy. He went there in 1904 and in between that year and 1910 he won the Championship four times.

He just failed in 1904. This was a year in which, though such scores were done as had hardly been dreamed of before, the Amateur Championship for once stole the thunder of the Open. Both Champion-ships were played on the same course, Sandwich, even as two years before both had been played at Hoylake, and 1904 at Sandwich will always be remembered as Travis's year, when the little middle-aged man from

America with the black cigar and the Schenectady
putter began the now almost too salutary process of
taking the national conceit out of us. As is sufficiently
well known Walter Travis was not socially a success
here, partly but by no means wholly through his own
fault. He was not a forthcoming person and seemed
to want chiefly to be left alone, but I do not think
that this altogether acquits us; my conscience tells
me that we ought to have tried harder to be friendly.

However that may be, perhaps because we did not
like him very much and he certainly did not like us at
all, I doubt if we have ever done full justice to him as
a golfer. The general belief now is that he won
because he holed putts 'all over the green.' He was
a magnificent putter and his putting during that
week was particularly deadly, but he had many other
merits as a player—a great mastery over all his clubs,
great accuracy and a complete knowledge of exactly
what he could do. Though a slight man with a rather
artificial style and no vast power, he seemed always
to have a little something up his sleeve. The hopes
that some of the carries at Sandwich would be just
too long for him were constantly being dashed: he
always just slipped over. Some of his spoon shots up
to the greens—he took a spoon where today people
would be taking a mashie-niblick—still remain in my
mind as models of beautiful precision. I do not think
that many of the amateurs realized how good he was,
but the professionals, some of whom arrived to see
the last two-days' play before the Open, were more
appreciative.

However, I must not let that rather sinister and
most formidable little figure lead me down a by-path,
seductive though it may be. I must return to James,
whose first summer at Walton brought him no great

triumph though it very nearly did. For the third time he had a putt for a 3 at the seventy-second hole to tie for the Championship; for the third time he could not quite hole it and had to be content with second place, on this occasion equal with Taylor. There was this time one truly poisonous ingredient in his cup of failure; when he holed his last putt he thought he had tied with Jack White, only to discover that a spectator had given him wrong information to the extent of just that one fatal stroke. We have several times heard vague stories of such mistakes and have not always perhaps believed them, but this one is given under James's own hand and seal in his book and that settles it. Put not your trust in spectators. Speaking as a watcher of many years I can give that advice from bitter experience. They have the best intentions no doubt but they are generally speaking unmitigated liars.

This Championship at Sandwich was as close and exciting a one as ever was played. I feel almost inclined to put forward a claim for that of 1911 on the same course as equally terrific; perhaps however it lacked something of the intensely dramatic quality of 1904 because the scoring in the last round was by no means so astonishingly low. This was the first year in which the winning score was below an average of 75 a round. The scores had been steadily coming down and at Prestwick the year before Vardon had done 300. Now Jack White brought the record down with a run to 296 and then only won with the skin of his teeth. It was a truly remarkable score, but it is right to add that the conditions were all in favour of low scoring. Sandwich was not the tremendous course it had been with the gutty, making by no means the same demand for great brassy play that had endeared it to Harry Vardon's heart. Moreover the weather had been fine and dry, the course had endured the trampling of many feet during the Amateur Championship a few days before, and was therefore playing very fast. Granted all these conditions however, the play was magnificent and the scoring on the second day such as had never been seen before.

Sandwich, as I said, had always been Harry Vardon's course; he had now emerged from his sanatorium and began as if he meant to win there again. This was the first year in which the number of entries was so large that only one round could be played on each of the first two days. Robert Thomson, who had succeeded James at Romford, a really good golfer, yet hardly one to be 'reckoned,' to use a word of John Ball's, as far as winning was concerned, led with 75. Then came Vardon and Jack Graham with 76, then Tom Vardon, Braid and Taylor with 77 apiece. Next day Vardon was at his very best with a 73 and led with 149, followed by Thomson 151, Graham 153, Sherlock 154, White and Taylor 155 and Braid 157. The general impression, which I fancy he shared himself, was that Vardon was on the way to victory.

In fact he was probably not yet strong enough for so fierce a strain and it was not long afterwards that he had a relapse and had for a while to retire again. Whatever the cause he played a really poor round on the morning of the last day and took 79. James meanwhile starting eight strokes behind him, a deficit which would once have seemed almost hopeless, came with a glorious spurt and a 69 to lead the field with 226. He reached the turn in 31 with a 3 at the long seventh hole and was, as far as I know, the first man ever to break 70 in an Open Championship though he did not have that record to himself for long. White, steadily improving, had played very, very well for 72 and he was now one behind James with 227 and one ahead of Vardon at 228. Taylor with a 74 was next with 229 and if ever the scene had appeared set for yet another victory for the Triumvirate, it did so now. Everybody knew Jack White was a fine golfer but hardly anyone thought he could win in a desperate finish against those three. He certainly had not the power or the accuracy or the confidence in driving of the very best, but this did not mean that he was not in the ordinary sense a good driver. He had plenty of dash and the fast ground helped him, and when it came to putting there was no one to teach him anything. He was a genuine artist on the greens, one who was not content with trying to hit the ball clean, and heaven knows most people find that hard enough; he was always ready, as John Low would have said, to play a stroke upon the green and wheedle the ball into the hole off the heel or the toe of his cleek. Beyond doubt he was a very fine putter and he had at Sandwich perfect greens on which to exercise his art.

It was not White but one another that the Triumvirate were watching that afternoon. However Jack, who started early, soon gave them an unpleasant reminder that he was not to be disregarded, for he reached the turn in 32. What was more, he showed no signs of breaking down on the way home. Just at the very end he became a little shaky and was twice in the rough during the last three holes, but he holed them bravely in 4 apiece and that made 69 and set up a fearful mark to aim at. Vardon cannot be said to have faded out; his 74 was good enough for a

sick man but not good enough when such a tune had
been played as had never been danced to before.
Jack White enduring the agonies of waiting for news
—and it took him a long time to get over it—must
have feared only Braid, who wanted a 70 to tie.
Taylor wanted 67 and that must have seemed un-
thinkable even to a man who can hardly believe that
the Fates will let him win.

James came first, still playing very finely and
reaching the turn in 36. He had no precise news as
to his competitors, for this was before the days of
field telephones and 'walkie-talkies' and players must
depend largely upon rumour; but he knew that with
the game he was playing he must finish there or there-
abouts. The first real news he got was from that
fatally inaccurate spectator, whose name no man
knows, who perhaps never knew himself the mischief
he had done. He said that White had finished in 70.
That meant that with four holes to play James needed
4, 3, 4, 4, strict par golf, to tie. The 3 came at the
fifteenth, which is a good enough 4 at all times, and
that made all the difference, for it gave him virtually
a stroke to play with. At the one-shot sixteenth he
was a little short with his tee shot. The hole was cut
at the back of the green with a bank behind it; a
putt played boldly past the hole might very likely
come back off the bank and lie dead. But this did
not seem a time for taking that risk; James was six
feet short with his second and missed the putt. Still
he had his two 4's, as he thought, to tie and no doubt
he further thought that once it came to a play-off
with Jack White he must win. The first 4 came at
the seventeenth—the hole was then at the bottom of
a deep hollow—and at the eighteenth he put his
second safely on the green, well up, some yards past

the hole. Now two putts would do it and he laid the first cautiously dead, a little short of the hole, popped the next one in and then discovered that White's score had been not 70 but 69. He had done a 71 and 140 for the day and it was just not good enough.

Meanwhile Taylor had set out on his last round determined to do or die and having his eye on Braid. He had such a start as a man could have only in a dream—3, 3, 2. Humanly speaking he must have gained three strokes on the whole field and victory was thinkable. He did drop a shot at the fourth but he was out in 32, where he was greeted with the news, true news this time, that it was no longer Braid he had to fear; the bursts of applause wafted across the course had not been only for him; White was the man and Taylor needed a 35 to tie with him. He started home as well as ever, 4, 4, 3, holed a long one for 4 at the Suez Canal, and when he came to the sixteenth tee he wanted, as Braid had wanted, 3, 4, 4 to tie. He was kept waiting a long time on that tee and played a bad tee shot but he hit the hole with his putt for 3. So he did at the seventeenth but the ball would not drop. At the home hole he was left with a ten-yard putt for his 3. 'A dusty, dry, dropper with a yard borrow from the right,' J. H. calls it in his book, and I think he would have liked to add one more epithet to that alliterative array. The ball touched the rim of the hole and that was 68 and he tied for second with Braid.

CHAPTER VI

The Great Foursome, 1905-1906

THE year 1905 was that of James's second win in
the Open Championship but it will be better
remembered in golfing history as the year of the great
foursome over four greens between England and
Scotland, Vardon and Taylor against Braid and Herd.
It was on a par with the matches of an older date, in
particular the famous foursome over three greens
between Allan Robertson and Tom Morris and the
Dunn brothers. I wish I could think that there will
ever be another like it again, but I see no prospect of
it at present, for as long as there is one long procession
of score-play tournaments with plenty of money to
be picked up in them, the professionals will not play
challenge matches. Nobody can conceivably blame
them, but one such foursome would be 'worth an
age without a name' of these eternal tournaments of
which the heart grows unutterably weary.

Exactly how the project began it is now hard to
say, but there was, I think, a general feeling that a real
fight would be a relief after so many exhibitions in
which everyone had beaten everybody else. The
backer for one side was obvious; Mr. (afterwards
Lord) Riddell was the big man at Walton Heath, a
great admirer of Braid's, with Scottish blood in his
veins; he would back Scotland; Mr. (later Sir
Edward) Hulton was ready to take England, and the
only question at first was who should be Braid's

partner. Willie Park was suggested, but he was too
busy and had perhaps had enough both of challenge
matches and of Harry Vardon; he declined and
Herd, the obvious choice from the beginning, got the
place. When the match was originally arranged no
one of the four was Champion but that was soon put
to rights by Braid winning at St. Andrews in July,
while the match was not to be played till September.
So let us take the Championship first.

This really ought to have been rather a dull
Championship with only one man, James, in the hunt.
Fortunately for those who like a little agony, that
one man elected, like the Fat Boy, to make their flesh
creep. He recovered wonderfully and won comfortably in the end, but only after a series of blood-curdling
events. He cannot be said to have been winning all
the time since at the end of the first two rounds Rowland Jones led him by a stroke, but that accomplished
and graceful golfer was hardly of the stature to hold
James for another thirty-six holes on St. Andrews
with its fierce homecoming. Taylor had had a bad
second round of 85, and Vardon, who ultimately
finished seventh, was already some way behind. It
looked like James's Championship and when he had
a very sound 78 for his third round he had gained
quite a useful lead which he promptly added to after
lunch. Cheered by the news that his most dangerous
enemy had had misfortunes he played as nearly as
might be perfectly till he had holed the long hole
home, the fourteenth, and now he was, barring
accidents, winning by the length of the street. He
was also however in the neighbourhood of the railway
and the railway was not what it is today, when the
player calmly drops or tees another ball and loses
stroke and distance. Then it was part of the course

and the player was in the Duke of Wellington's words 'In a d——d awkward predicament and must get out of it as best he could.' Rails, iron chairs, sleepers —what a possibility of knotted horrors was his!

At the fifteenth James cut his second on to the railway and duly got it out at the first attempt; but the ball hit a man and bounded off him nearly into bush; result a 6. One would have thought that having escaped so cheaply from the railway once, even this dashing young blade of five and thirty would have avoided it at the next hole. Not a bit of it; he hit a tremendous drive carrying the Principal's Nose and pitching into the little bunker beyond it called Deacon Sime. If the ball had lain badly he would have dug it out safely; but it lay pretty well, he became in his own words 'too venturesome,' went for the green and was on the railway again. From this point I will quote him from *Advanced Golf*: 'I found it lying in a horrible place, being tucked up against one of the iron chairs in which the rails rest, it was on the left-hand side of the right-hand rail, playing towards the hole, and the only crumb of comfort was that it was not on the other side of either of the rails. I took my niblick and tried to hook it out, but did not succeed, the ball moving only a few yards, and being in much the same position against the rail. With my fourth, however, I got it back on the course, but in a very difficult position. It went some thirty yards past the hole, near to the bunker on the left of the second green. As the ground was, I had only about a yard to come and go on with a run-up shot, which was plainly the proper stroke to play in the circumstances if I wanted to get close to the hole, as I must do if I was to get a 6. It was a bold and very risky shot to play, but I played it and it came off, the ball running dead and thus I got my 6. In all the four rounds of that Championship I think it was the best shot that I played.'

Even so this had been rather a shattering series of experiences immediately before playing the Road hole, of all holes in the world, but he played it gaily and finished five strokes ahead of Rowland Jones and Taylor. His score was 318, twenty-two strokes higher than Jack White's score of the year before and yet he won by five strokes and White had only won by a single one. Figures can be most delusive things. After it was all over the winner reflected that in the circumstances it might have been wiser to lift the ball at the sixteenth under a penalty of two strokes and tee it. It is a great comfort that he did not for we should have lost an incomparable shot and an intensely dramatic moment.

The great foursome, by far the greatest match that I can recall in point of popular interest, was set to begin at St. Andrews in September. Each side had chosen two courses, the Scotsmen St. Andrews and Troon, the Englishmen St. Anne's and Deal. I think, though this may be only English partisanship, that Vardon and Taylor were on the whole the favourites, but one thing is perfectly certain, nobody expected on either side such a landslide of holes as overwhelmed the Scottish pair at Troon. We believed that it would be 'a' through a braw fecht atweens' as Tom Morris said of his famous match against the Dunns. That either side could gain fourteen holes in one day's play was never dreamed of, and perhaps if the match could have been played from then till the crack of doom such a thing would never have happened again. However, happen it did; 'it's no possible but it's a fact' in Ben Sayers's words; and when half the match was over it was in effect finished.

There was an enormous crowd at St. Andrews, 10,000, it was thought, in the morning and more in the afternoon. The score was announced to them by the raising of a blue flag if England won a hole, a yellow one if Scotland won, and both flags for a half. A Scottish crowd is not very easily controlled and does not restrain its patriotic emotions. This crowd, according to *Golf Illustrated*, was 'no worse and perhaps a little better than expected,' with the significant corollary that 'there is no excuse for cheering when the player is suffering from the mortification of a short putt.' It was worse than Harry Vardon expected. Taylor has told in his book and has repeated to me since by word of mouth that his partner was so irritated by what he thought the unfairness of the spectators that he several times declared he would have no more of it and would walk in. This was the more surprising because Vardon had as a rule showed himself so astonishingly tranquil and unruffled, no matter what the crowd might be. Taylor persuaded him to think better of it and the play duly went on, but the revenge of Troon must have been all the sweeter.

Before play began the referee, John Low, seems to have asked the players to be careful about the rule as to 'brushing lightly with the hand across the putt.' This was no doubt on account of an unfortunate incident that had happened just before in the final of the Calcutta Cup, when one player was penalized by the umpires who held that he had smoothed down a rough place on the green whereas he declared he had only brushed away a loose impediment. *Golf Illustrated* declares that the players were punctiliously careful accordingly and always looked to the referee for his sanction. Taylor however does not particularly recall this and perhaps the matter was over-emphasized in the description of the play.

James with the honour drove the first ball for Scotland, and Taylor followed for England. The play was on the whole very good in the trying circumstances and we are told that in particular James's approach putting with his aluminium club was excellent. All day long Scotland were going ahead to be pulled back, but they ended two up. They drew first blood at the second hole, were pulled back to square at the fifth, won the eighth and ninth and turned two up. Down to one at the thirteenth, back to two up again at the long hole when they had a fine 4, three up at the fifteenth, and so, with a stymie to help them at the sixteenth, three up at lunch. After lunch the Englishmen played very well out and squared at the eighth. So far they were one under fours, but Vardon missed a putt at the ninth. Scotland were one up again and went farther ahead with a 3 at the tenth and a 2 at the High Hole. England lost the thirteenth as well, won the next two, lost the sixteenth, won the seventeenth, where Herd bunkered his second, and so ended only two down after all. The crowd carried its heroes off the course in triumph, and J. H. murmured to his partner that you would think the match was finished already.

After that Troon and the deluge. There was no metaphorical cloud in the sky to warn the great West of Scotland crowd of the terrible things to come. To be sure Herd began by missing a short putt but that was recovered and all went tolerably well till the sixth hole. Then suddenly came disaster. The Englishmen played tremendously and the Scots became timid with their approach putts and made no amends with the short ones: the putts were really short and they missed them. So the astounding thing had happened that by lunch time England was six up on the day and four up on the match. And there was no slackening afterwards; the slaughter went on without rest and without mercy. Vardon and Taylor started with two 3's and that was the sort of golf they were playing; an iron or cleek shot near the hole and down went the putt. So in the end they were fourteen up on the day and twelve up on the match. Braid was not feeling very well and Herd had a sore knee that made him wince, but they made no excuses and the rout was altogether beyond excuse. There is no doubt that the Englishmen played just as well as they ever had or could, and the crowd, though naturally depressed, treated them well. It is a comfort when a player says what he really thinks about his own game and so we may be grateful for Vardon's comment in his book: 'I personally have never seen such a brilliant exhibition of the game as we produced on this occasion.' 'J. H.' I said to the surviving partner at Westward Ho! the other day, 'you must have played terribly well.' 'Well, yes, we did,' he answered. I never spoke to the other side about the match and cannot tell what they said.

In effect it was all over but the Scottish pair made a most courageous come-back at St. Anne's in the following week. They had a shocking start and became fifteen down. Then at the tenth Herd holed a long putt and from that moment he putted splendidly and both he and James really began to play. They had lopped off four holes by lunch and were still eleven down. In the afternoon they piled on the agony and were only six down with one to play but lost that last hole. Seven down was a dreadful mill-stone but there was still some spark of life left in the match.

The match nearly had a deplorable ending. Vardon's health had naturally given some anxiety but so far all had been well. Now he had a bad haemorrhage on the night before the last day's play at Deal. Taylor thought he would be unable to play and next morning was one of violent wind and driving rain. However, Vardon felt better and when he and his partner had won the first two holes he doubtless felt better still. An interesting little light is thrown on the weather and also to some extent on the differences that clubs and balls have made in the game, differences so hard for the modern players to appreciate that I must be forgiven for rubbing them in. Most people will remember the old fourth hole, the Sandy Parlour, at Deal and will think of it in normal circumstances as a mashie-niblick or at most a mashie shot. The wind was so strong that Vardon specially mentions his cleek shot to the green to get a par 3 and win the hole. The two Englishmen played, in very different conditions, almost as well as they had at Troon. A 79 in the morning made them thirteen up and they won by 13 and 12. They had shown themselves a very great pair, and now after all these years I think it may be said that they were unquestionably better as a pair than their adversaries, fitting in their respective shots the more deftly and having the greater confidence in one another.

It had been a bad beating and I suppose that a little something of bitterness always arose in the remembrance but James was of a disposition at once too placid and too determined to let it affect his game. As far as he had lost any of his championship glory he soon regained it by winning his second *News of the World*. In 1904 Taylor had not failed to win on his own course, Mid-Surrey, and now it was James's turn at Walton Heath. Not that it is always wholly an advantage to be playing at home, for a professional on his own course feels some of the obligations of a host; James was intensely conscientious about the course and would be out early and late to see that nothing had been forgotten. In fact he did win and, after he had surmounted the first hurdle, comfortably enough, but his opening match against Sandy Herd was touch and go. The two had met at Mid-Surrey the year before when Herd won at the nineteenth, the first match in this tournament that I ever watched. Now they were drawn together in the first round at Walton and again it went beyond the home green. It ought not to have if Braid could have holed a fairly short putt on either of the last two greens. However he made amends by getting down a good one for a 3 at the nineteenth.

In the final he met Harry Vardon's younger brother Tom. Tom Vardon, who later went to America and died there, was a very fine, dashing golfer, of a cheerful character, who took the game more lightheartedly than his brother. He was not a pretty player, with his right thumb down the shaft and a perceptible lift—it might be called a jump—in his up swing. But he was uncommonly good, quite how good perhaps only those knew who played with him regularly at Sandwich. They thought unutterable things of him. He got a good start against James—two up at the fourth hole, which he won in 4 after being a long way wide of the green in 2 while James had an eminently holeable putt for 3 and mysteriously took 5. But to play thirty-six holes against James at Walton was like playing Zeus on his home course on Olympus, and sure enough James was two up at lunch and won at the fifteenth hole in the afternoon. So he retired to his winter quarters with a cheering victory to make up for Troon, and a handsome testimonial from Walton Heath to celebrate the Championship.

1906 began with a new tournament, the London Foursomes, which was the forerunner of the present London Amateur Foursomes. A club could be represented by its professional and one amateur or by two amateurs. There were from the start two pairs, one of which seemed, humanly speaking, sure to win, James and Herbert Fowler for Walton Heath, J. H. Taylor and Sidney Fry for Mid-Surrey. Both lived up to expectations and more or less trampled their way through to the final which was due to be played at Walton Heath. It was an excellent match on paper but Sidney Fry had match-playing virtues not so liberally given to his amateur adversary and Mid-Surrey won by 9 and 8.

In 1906 the Championship had come round again to Muirfield where James had won five years before. Of all the Championships in which the Triumvirate showed their quality I think none was more notable than this one, for they were left well behind to start with, but the audacious leaders all 'came back to their horses,' leaving the last round to be again a battle between the three inevitables. To begin with all three took 77, whereas Jack Graham had done a wonderful 71: Bobbie Maxwell, entrenched on his own course where he was so infinitely formidable, did a 73 and so did a young man called George Duncan, not yet twenty-three years old, a little temperamental perhaps but brimful of golf, as no one with eyes could fail to see. Braid blamed himself for coming down far too early to the course and hanging about waiting for his time, which was a late one, and hearing about other people's scores. It is never a wise thing to do and may almost be said to have wrecked poor Abe Mitchell's championship career once and for all at Deal in 1920.

The second day saw something of a general post. Taylor now went to the top of the tree with an extraordinary round of 72, with a 31 home that ended with a 5. Jack Graham had wasted some of his first day's good work by taking 79 and he was second with 150, one shot behind Taylor, and equal with Harry Vardon who had done a 73. Maxwell and Duncan were 151 apiece and James 153. He had played well up to the green and hit his putts well when he got there, but they would not drop; so he philosophically reflected that they would probably drop next day. The draw for the last day saw Taylor out fairly early; Vardon came two or three holes behind him and Braid was to bring up the rear with the good or bad fortune of knowing what he had to do. One thing that may have affected the result was that J. H. and Jack Graham were drawn together and I do not think J. H. liked it. He had the greatest admiration for his partner, alike as a man and a golfer, but playing shot for shot against him all day long and striving with might and main not to be beaten by an amateur was not perhaps best suited to his score-playing temperament. He had enough to do to beat himself and the Fates, without this additional trial. He fought the good fight up to his 3 at the very last hole of the second round, but I think Jack had very nearly killed him.

Nevertheless with a round to go he led the field

with 224. Rowland Jones was 225 and Vardon and
Braid 227. James had been very steady and good
and the putts had begun to drop and 74 kept him well
in the hunt. Now he had to wait till Taylor had
almost finished before he set out on his last round.
When it came the news was most refreshing to the
spirits. With two holes to go Taylor could hardly
do better than 81 (with that 3 he in fact did 80) and
Vardon, it seemed, could not do much better. Rowland Jones had ruined himself with 83, even as Duncan
had in the morning. Jack Graham was two strokes
behind Taylor. James wanted a 76 to win, and
playing as he was, he knew he ought to do it. He
had a cheering start for his tee shot to the first hole
finished on the second tee and he got his 3 after all.
38 out was sound and steady, but it did not leave much
margin against a rainy day. A good putt or two
were badly wanted to make sure and they duly came,
one at the eleventh and another at the twelfth. Now
he was 'sailing with supreme dominion.' Hole after
hole was done in the par score. It was all over bar
the shouting with two holes to go and then he holed
a vast putt for 3 at the seventeenth. My *Golf
Illustrated* tells me that James had 'a happy half-smile
all the way.' If so it must have now become almost
a grin for he had a 7 to win. He duly got a 4 for 35
home, 73 for the round and 300 for the four rounds.
His figures home are worth setting down for those
who remember Muirfield as it was. 4, 4, 4, 4, 3, 4, 5,
3, 4—eight holes in par and one hole a stroke better.
A more faultless piece of finishing it would be hard
to imagine.

This year saw the moving of the *News of the World*
tournament from London to the Provinces. Apparently it was not regarded as a success as it was

never played away from a London course again till
forty years later at Hoylake. The move in 1906 was
to a very good course, Hollinwell near Nottingham,
sandy, heathery and altogether engaging. The
tournament was thoroughly interesting and almost
iconoclastic in result. For one thing, no one of the
Triumvirate won, though, to be sure, Sandy Herd
bobbed up to uphold the honour of the elder school.
For another, insurgent youth really made itself felt,
in particular George Duncan, who had the temerity
to beat James on his way to the semi-final, and Charles
Mayo who climbed one peak higher and reached
the final. I need not describe Duncan or his
fascinating game for he has for years been a familiar
figure, but Mayo needs a word perhaps since he has
long been in America and the golfer of today hardly
remembers him. It was his holing of all manner of
putts that chiefly took him into the final at Hollinwell
where he was not in the least expected, but he was a
considerable golfer in other ways. He had no great
physique or apparent strength and his rather exagger-
ated turn of the body hardly inspired confidence;
but a good player he was and one who became unquestionably better and stronger after this first success,
although perhaps by some mysterious rule of compensation he ceased to hole so many long putts.

The success of these two young men, Duncan and
Mayo, no doubt encouraged them in a bold project,
that of throwing down the gauntlet to Braid and
Vardon for a seventy-two-hole foursome. The
general view was that it was over-bold and I hardly
imagine that the challengers themselves believed they
would win, but it would at any rate give them valuable experience and bring them more prominently
to the fore. Today the promising young professional

has a long string of tournaments throughout the summer in which to try to fulfil his promise, but it was not so in 1906. There were few tournaments and the exhibition match business went all or nearly all into a very few select hands. So something in the nature of an adventure was needed by ambitious youth.

The match attracted plenty of interest and there was a big crowd to see the first half of it at Walton Heath. Indeed there is always a crowd on that heath which is free to all the world and his wife, and also to his dog. Youth came excellently out of its ordeal on the other man's course and did as well as anyone could have expected in finishing only four down. Vardon in his book tells one interesting thing about the game. The green of the famous short sixth was so keen that it was almost impossible to stop the ball on it. Vardon therefore deliberately put his partner into the left-hand bunker, the bunker nearest the flag, in the sure and certain hope that James would play one of his earth-shaking explosion shots which should drop the ball spent and lifeless close to the hole. His confidence was not misplaced for they had the hole in 3 in both rounds.

The second half of the match was played at Timperley near Manchester, which was then Duncan's course. It was perhaps too much to hope that this would seriously affect the result, but in the morning age only gained one hole. In the afternoon it drew right away to win by 9 and 8. Both Vardon and Braid had played really well throughout: they had upheld their position and honour may be said to have been satisfied all round. Three years later Duncan and Mayo had made another attack on that jealously guarded fortress of the elder school and encountered

Braid and Taylor, with no better success as it turned out; but we must come to that in due order. They also played Ray and Tom Vardon over seventy-two holes in 1908 and beat them, playing very fine golf as I can personally testify for I saw them. These foursomes were full of interest and one can only wish once again that the old spirit of challenge was not in abeyance.

CHAPTER VII

The Greatest Championship of All, 1907-1909

IN looking back at it 1907 seems a year of long-drawn-out fight between France, represented by Arnaud Massy, and the embattled forces of Britain. France had beyond all question the best of it in 1907 and Britain got its own back when the struggle was continued in 1908. Walter Travis had given our national complacency a shake by winning the Amateur Championship in 1904, but nobody had dreamed, least of all the professionals, that our Open Championship was in any danger from an invader. And yet Massy had given his proofs and I think there were individuals among the professionals who realized that he must be treated with respect. He had learnt his golf among the Atlantic winds of Biarritz and then had been sent by Sir Everard Hambro to polish up his golfing education at North Berwick. Here he and Ben Sayers naturally became well acquainted and Ben, who was always emphatic and enthusiastic, as was his nephew Jack White, was unwearied in singing the Frenchman's praises.

Massy was beyond all question a grand golfer and a splendid figure of a man. It was something of a pose on his part not to know the Basque language, but if he was French on his father's side he was undoubtedly Basque on his mother's and had all the formidable air of that athletic race. He was well armed at all points of the game and in particular a putter with a lovely delicate touch. If he lacked anything it was the stolidity of his British rivals. Courage he certainly did not lack, but he was a player of moods and could now and then grow careless or dejected if he deemed the Fates against him. He had a fine, rollicking, rapscallion way with him. Whether he was telling of his experiences as a bomb-thrower at Verdun or of his despoiling opulent Spaniards at Nivelle, he was admirable company and everybody was fond of him.

Massy, now about twenty-nine years old, had won the French Open Championship at La Boulie with a fine score in the previous year. In the February of 1907 most of the British leaders had met him in the Grand Duke Michael's tournament at Cannes, and he had beaten them all with some comfort. In fact they had been warned as Taylor had been in his match with Vardon at Ganton ten years before. James was under no illusions about him and on being asked for a forecast as to the Championship he named three besides the Triumvirate, Massy, Pulford and Tom Vardon. It was an inspired piece of prophecy for Massy won and Pulford and Tom Vardon tied for third place.

Braid having won for the last two years came to Hoylake the favourite but was deposed from that perhaps uncomfortable honour after the qualifying rounds. The qualifiers were divided between two days and on the first Massy had two very fine rounds of 73 and 75. On the second day Taylor led with 76 and 78, equally good scores since the weather had become more difficult. When the real thing began there was a gale blowing from the west with heavy rain. Taylor according to *Golf Illustrated* described the weather as 'heart-breaking and nerve-racking' and he certainly was not one to make a pother about a puff of wind.

Massy got away to a grand start in the weather that he loved with a 76. He was not quite so deadly in the afternoon for he took 81 and Taylor and Tom Ball were within a stroke of him.

James had for him a lamentable day of it, taking 82 and 85. The 85 included an 8 at the notorious Briars, the sixth, which was once halved in 9 in the final of the Amateur Championship; nor was his the only 8 there, for it was a terrible hole that day. There is a story that James broke his braces in the course of the day which would certainly not help him, but I can find no confirmation of so intimate a detail, and it may well be legendary.

He was ten strokes behind the leaders, in an apparently hopeless position even as he had been in Sandy Herd's year when there was nothing for it but to go out for everything. He made a brave try; he was not driving as steadily as usual and was once more out of bounds at the Briars but he finished in 75. In the afternoon he looked likely to do better still until he missed a short putt for a 2 at the Rushes (the thirteenth) and then drove into a ditch at the Field and took 6, which was the end of all things. A 76 gave him a total of 318, just six too many.

Meanwhile, Massy and Taylor had been having a desperate race of it. Massy had not weakened in the least with his 78, but Taylor had got his nose in front with a fine 76. The general impression was that it was an old horse for a hard road and that J. H. would do it again. But at the third hole (the Long) he pushed out his tee shot, tried too much with his next and got under the cop below the out-of-bounds bank. He took 7 to the hole and never quite got over it. With 77 against Taylor's 80 Massy won by two shots.

His victory seemed to call for a little friendly revenge and a British storming party set out to attack him in the French Open Championship at La Boulie. Even James was persuaded to overcome his well-grounded horror of the sea. It was no new one since Ralph Smith says that even as a boy at home he regularly declined to use the ferry. Taylor too has assured me that when they sailed from Campbeltown to play at Islay, James's sufferings were really pathetic and during the whole voyage he lay more or less unconscious of his surroundings. He never got over this weakness and often felt sick even in a drive of any length in a car. No wonder he preferred dry land, but there was this in addition; he was afraid of the bright hot light of the Riviera for his eyes, and this probably had also something to do with his resolute refusal to go to America. However, his patriotism triumphed; with a strong band of crusaders he set out for France and Massy was again too much for them on his own course. On the first day he and Braid were equal at the head of the list at 149 with Vardon two strokes behind. Next morning Massy had a 74 to James's 76 and Vardon killed himself with 79. A 75 in the afternoon was good enough for Massy to win. James was three behind him and that was not good enough even for second place, for Jean Gassiat came with a wet sheet and a great last round of 72. France had the first two places and the crusade had failed.

After that came a domestic interlude in the shape of the *News of the World* tournament at Sunningdale, which ended in James's third victory in five years. In *Advanced Golf* James declared that the golf all round had been of a definitely higher standard than ever before in any tournament and that after the first nine holes in the first round he himself had stuck to an average of 4's. He was never thoroughly hard put to it except against Taylor in the final and he got away from him in the end. Coburn by 3 and 2, Gray by 6 and 4, Edmundson by 6 and 5 and Ray by 4 and 2—those were his victims on the way. Taylor just beat Vardon in the semi-final and in the final he and James were all square at lunch. The issue was really decided at the short thirteenth hole in the afternoon. James had hooked his tee shot into rough country and Taylor seemed to have a certain 3 and a chance of a 2. James's ball lay well and he put it ruthlessly dead; Taylor went rather boldly for the hole and missed coming back. After that James won by 4 and 2.

There was to be one more French and English or rather Scottish battle before the year closed and one more triumph for France. James and Massy were matched to play thirty-six holes at Deal. The match was played only a few days before Christmas but the weather was on its best winter behaviour. To begin with there was only one in it and it seemed that the old champion was going to give the new one a terrible dressing, for Braid was four up in less than no time, and four up, as some acute philosopher has observed, is much more than three. However, Massy stuck to his guns nobly; he was playing his mashie in a manner worthy of North Berwick and James let a putt or two slip. He was still three up at the sixteenth, but lost both the last two holes and it was virtually all to play for. The first hole after lunch was dramatic in the extreme. Both were duly on the green in two but Massy's ball was behind a nasty bump. Green or no green he took his mashie, pitched his ball over the bump and it ran on into the hole for a 3. That was all square and he never looked back; he was two up at the turn, dormy three and won at the seventeenth. What a year of it he had had!

1908 opened with a renewal of these international matches but now the tide of battle turned with a vengeance. In the early spring the Triumvirate were again invited to play in several Riviera tournaments in which both Massy and Gassiat were to play, and James once more braved the terrors of the Channel in the good cause. First came a tournament at Nice. This course, at Cagnes, on which I played a few years later had, as I remember it, engaging olive groves and fine velvety greens. The standard of greens in the Riviera can hardly be high considering what they must suffer in the torrid summer, but these were excellent judged by any standard. Apart from them the golf was undistinguished. Vardon won here with 143, four strokes better than Massy, with James and Gassiat equal third a stroke behind him. On the next day there was a match between Britain and France, Baptiste Bomboudiac making the third Frenchman. Britain won all along the line, Braid beating Massy, Taylor Gassiat and Vardon Bomboudiac.

Next the three went to Hyères, a pretty rather than a good course on which the chief hazards used to be hurdles, unless I do it an injustice, though I remember one charming hole down a glade between silver birches. Here Taylor came in first, winning not only the first prize but a vast silver trophy, the Tatler Cup. I think this must have been the one occasion on which J. H. has told me he saw James really let himself go. The Cup having been filled by the winner, James danced a reel to the general admiration. 'I can see his long legs now,' said J. H. From Hyères was the briefest of journeys to Costebelle for which I have an old affection since it was the first place at which I stayed and the first golf course on which I played in the Riviera. I rather doubt if it exists any longer. This must have been the first of the two courses that were made there, near the Colline des Oiseaux; quite a good course it was, neither very short nor very easy. Here Vardon won again with 152 with Massy second, James third and Taylor fourth.

The British retaliation for 1907 did not end there. A match was made between Massy and Vardon to be played at Deal where Massy had rounded off his triumphs the year before by beating Braid. I was then in process of shaking off the shackles of the law and so went down to Deal to see the match. I still remember the thrill of setting out by an early morning train with something of the romantic sensations of one driving into the country for a prize fight, Hazlitt perhaps on his way to watch Bill Neate and the Gaslight Man, or Borrow going to see Ned Paynter knock out Tom Oliver.

Journeys to see golf matches have become more commonplace since then but there is still a definite and peculiar romance belonging to some of them. Perhaps in later days I have come to love best of all the night journey to St. Andrews, with breakfast as the train crosses the Forth Bridge, the stepping out into the brisk, cool air at Leuchars and the first view of the links as the train comes winding its way from Guardbridge. But in those times I think that for me the pleasant, leisurely train to Sandwich and Deal, with the change at Minster, was the best of all and indeed I love it very much still, though there is now no change at Minster to give that added poignancy. For a change just before the last lap, by delaying our arrival and lengthening our rapture of expectation, does add something, and it so happens that some of the best and most famous of links possess just such an exciting halt, on the very verge of paradise. There is Leuchars, as I say, on the way to St. Andrews, and on the West we change at Kilmarnock for Prestwick and Troon. There is Ashford, change for Rye, and Preston, change for St. Anne's; we must get out at Lime Street and cross to Central before the beloved haven of Hoylake is reached.

However this is a shameless digression from my road to Deal for the great match. I had, as I have described, seen Vardon just after he had won his first Championship but that had been eleven years before; his fame had vastly increased since and I had never seen him again. There was a considerable change from the lean young man I had seen at Ganton in trousers and a flannel jacket. Vardon had grown considerably stouter, during his stays at the Sanatorium, and had long worn the knickerbocker suit which had once been deemed something in the nature of an upheaval of social laws. Moreover if his style in those early days had seemed so heterodox as to be almost ugly, it was now a monument of ease and beauty. How much the change was in the player himself and how much in the eyes of the beholder I do not know, but certainly from that day at Deal I was the most fervent admirer.

The thrill of Vardon and of the crowd, for there was a surprisingly big crowd so far from London, and the general sensation of excitement, which has grown more familiar since then, had to make up between them the delights of the day, for the match was a poor one. Vardon went right away from the start, playing very fine accurate golf in a stiff wind, won four out of the first five holes, was six up at lunch and finally won the match by 9 and 7. It was one of Massy's bad days; for once in a while he could not putt and ever and anon he would look up in mute despair, calling on high heaven to witness his failure.

Later in the year Braid rubbed it into Massy and had a little private revenge for Deal on his own account. The match was at Acton, and I am bound to confess that I remember little of the course but much of the hotness of the day. The match took a converse course to that at Deal. Even as Massy had early been four down there so James was now, but he pulled himself together and pulled the holes back so quickly that he was two up at lunch and won by 5 and 4. As he also beat Massy by 10 and 9 at Warwick he had certainly got some of his own back.

Nor was poor Massy much more fortunate in the Open Championship at Prestwick, but he was always something of an *aut Caesar aut nullus* golfer, and when after three steady rounds he found himself eight strokes behind James he may well have realized that the game was up, so that he did not try very hard in his final 81. Indeed if ever there was a one-man Championship, this was it. From the very start Braid was winning and his golf reached its very highest peak. Up till now Jack White's 296 at Sandwich, made admittedly in favourable conditions, had never been approached; James's 300 at Muirfield came nearest to it and if a pundit were asked to prophesy before a Championship as to the winning score, it was the right thing to say that four 75's would take a great deal of beating; nor was the speaker likely to find anyone to bet to the contrary. And now here came this audacious James with 291, only three over an average of 4's. It was hardly credible; it was certainly not decent.

Here again the conditions were perfect for scoring. The greens might have been too fast but for a deluge of rain (which caused the professional international match to be abandoned) so that the ball could be boldly pitched up to the hole on those rather small Prestwick greens, while at the same time there was plenty of run through the green. The weather on the first day was fine, hot and still, and if there was some breeze on the second day and the greens had grown faster, the conditions were yet decidedly favourable. Granting all this however James's golf was entirely magnificent. He dominated the tournament from beginning to end, serene, majestic and inevitable. And this score of his such as nobody had ever dreamed of before, contained one of the most superfluous blots, his eight at the Cardinal in the third round, that ever marred a card. As it seemed to me his hitting of the ball all through was entirely perfect and his putting at those telling middle distances most deadly.

It would not be pedantically accurate to say that James led from the start but in effect he did. The best score in the first round was a 68, a wonderfully fine score too, by Ernest Gray from Littlehampton; but though Gray was always a player capable of a sparkling round, he could never have clung to James for four rounds, and in fact his next three scores were 79, 83, 81. So what mattered was that James had begun by opening up a very perceptible gap between himself and all his most dangerous rivals. He started with a 3 at that hole along the railway which is always perilous and once cost Willie Fernie a 9 in the first round of a Championship. He had his orthodox 3 at the little second and turned in 33. Coming home he had a few 5's but ended as he had begun with two 3's and that was 70. His second round opened more quietly—4, 4, 5—but then he went on with four 3's in a row and again took 33 to the turn. Coming home he had a really terrific 3 at the twelfth, where there was then a stone wall across the course guarding the green and the only respectable thing to do, the only thing that ordinarily good players could do, was to play short in two and so home with a pitch. However James, having hit a vast tee shot, had other ideas. He walked a long way forward, taking a very deliberate view of the scenery, and then—I can see him now—returned to his ball at a slow, shambling run. He hit a glorious brassy shot right home and holed the putt. He rather spoilt the effect of this stupendous effort by taking 6 at the thirteenth, the Sea Hedrig, but promptly put that to rights again with yet one more 3 at the Goose-Dubs. Another 70 seemed easily within his reach but he finished almost mildly 5, 4, 5, 4. Even so with 142 he led Gray by five strokes, Herd and David Kinnell by six and Tom Ball by seven. He must be going to win, and then at the Cardinal, the third hole in the third round, came that 8, and after that his position was rather stronger than before.

As I saw that 8, with my eyes nearly starting out of my head, and as I venture to think it was the one thoroughly ill-judged hole from beginning to end that I ever saw him play, I will describe it with some minuteness. I was standing by the huge Cardinal bunker waiting for his tee shot to arrive and did not see what club he used, but I gather from the *Golf Illustrated* account that it was an iron. If so, this was probably an unnecessary bit of caution to be followed by a series of rash acts. He cut the ball into the rough and was still a good long way back from the huge cross-bunker. He went for the carry—this I think was rather unwise—and was promptly caught in the bunker, his ball lying near the boarded face. He could not possibly have reached the green and —this was still more unwise—he took his mashie to try to gain distance. The ball hit the boards and glanced off at an angle into the Pow Burn on the right, out of bounds. Again he took his mashie and exactly the same thing happened, amid a deathly, horror-stricken silence. The next time he was content to take a niblick and dig the ball out; he was on the green in 6, where he ought to have been in 4 at most, and two putts made 8.

The writer in *Golf Illustrated*, as one proud of great men's confidences, made the interesting revelation that he 'happened to know that Braid was annoyed with himself.' I don't doubt that he was, but no one in the crowd waiting for him by the fourth green with no knowledge of the disaster, could have guessed it as they saw him advancing at precisely his usual steady, leisurely pace, with no slightest mark of emotion on his face. The only sign of any disturbance was that he took three putts on the fourth green, and then at the next, the Himalayas, he holed a putt for a 2 and he was back in his stride, out in 39, home in 38 and 77 after all. David Kinnell had gained three strokes on him but James could well afford that and more. Tom Ball had gained a mere one stroke and Sandy Herd had positively lost two: it was, in the American language, 'in the bag.' A great crowd of patriots went out in the afternoon to bring home the winner. If they felt any uneasiness at the Cardinal it was soon over for James had it in 4, for the first time in the four rounds. His play all through was a model of steady brilliance, 36 each way and a 72. Tom Ball was second with 299, next came Ray and after him Herd. 'I 'ate heights,' Tom Vardon used to say and I have often wished James had not had that one, but it would have been a dull Championship without it and even with it, it was almost dull. He was too good.

James had now caught up Harry Vardon with a record of four Championships and was temporarily ahead of Taylor with his three. He was cock of the walk, but he did not win the *News of the World* tournament this time. It was to be played at Mid-Surrey again, where Taylor always staked out a strong claim. The two met in the first round and out went James, beaten after a good match by 2 and 1. The feature of the tournament was the ever memorable final between Taylor and Robson, the almost unknown young man with the red head from Bromborough, who hit the ball vast distances, not always perhaps rigidly straight. This outrageous young gentleman was actually three up on J. H. on his own course at lunch; he was three down at the turn in the afternoon; he got two of those three back but not the third and lost a great match by two holes. Sherlock was one of the semi-finalists and Mayo was the other. The honour of the Triumvirate was left solely in J. H.'s hands and he did not betray the trust. All things are comparative and 1909 was almost a poor year for James, for he won neither the Open Championship nor the *News of the World*, which was played on his own course at Walton Heath. He was second in the Championship and won a challenge foursome match, but just at this time he seemed so nearly invincible that it was a definite shock when he did not win. To be sure the Championship was this year in England and it is a remarkable fact that James never succeeded in winning one out of his native country. He was within a putt of doing so more than once, but he needed apparently the 'snell' breezes of Scotland to waft him to complete victory.

The Championship was played at Deal for the first time, an honour which that noble course well deserved. There can be no fiercer test than the home-coming there against a wind and if there is possibly a slight element of chance over the approaches to the last four holes, it is a poor heart that never rejoices over a little luck and they are truly fascinating holes. Taylor has always been credited with the statement that the only way to win a Championship is to win it easily. He is not prepared to admit that he ever made it, but he heartily agrees with it and no one has ever lived up to it better. He did so this time at Deal and though James and Tom Ball tied for second place and played very fine golf, there was really only one in it. As between J. H. and James the first round did it and in more ways than one. It sent J. H. off in that unbeatable mood of his that arose from a bad start brilliantly atoned for. It left James too many strokes behind, strokes that it was humanly speaking impossible to get back with J. H. well away and set for victory. If any one hole did it more than another it was the tenth in Taylor's first round. He had played splendidly in the qualifying rounds but now all went ill. Clouds gathered on his brow and it would indeed have been a brave spectator who should ask him how he was getting on. He took 41 to the turn, too many by far considering the fine weather and general low scoring. Then at the tenth hole—I saw it and remember it well—he holed a putt for 3 and, metaphorically, the sky was blue once more, the sun shone and the birds sang. Three years before at Muirfield he had gone out in 41, holed a putt for 3 at the tenth and come home in a miraculous 31. This time he was not quite so overwhelming but he came home in 33 which, heaven knows, was good enough, and so was 74 for the round. James was also out in 41, with 6's at the second and fifth, but he was not home in 33. He was home in 38 and five strokes behind J. H. After that the two may have been said to have played if not shot for shot, at any rate round for round: J. H. had 73, 74, 74 and James 75, 73, 74. There was no getting those shots back and James tied with Tom Ball for second place with 301, six shots behind J. H. with 295. Johns, the surprise of the tournament, who had begun with a 72, was fourth and Vardon far down the list with 316. So J. H. had caught up the other two at four Championships apiece.

The *News of the World* at Walton Heath saw the first really successful revolt against the domination of the elder school. Braid and Taylor went out in the very first round, Vardon survived to the semi-final to lose by a hole to Herd and Herd was thoroughly beaten in the final by Tom Ball. James not only lost his first match to Jack Rowe but lost it by 4 and 3. Exactly what happened I do not now remember for, to tell the truth, I had imagined that I should have other opportunities of watching James and the notion of his losing on his own course had not occurred to me. I was told that Rowe had played very fine golf and had well and truly beaten the great man, and there I must leave it. I do vividly remember Taylor losing at the twentieth hole to Hepburn. After their tee shots to that hole the agitated referee could not decide whose play it was and proposed to walk all the way to the hole, some 200 yards up a slope, to see if he could tell better from there. J. H. bade him 'for heaven's

sake say something, sir' or words to that effect and
the poor man made up his mind at last.

The final was a remarkable match since it began
with ten holes halved in a row. Then Herd won one
but he did not win many more for Tom Ball sailed
away triumphantly to win by 7 and 5. Tom Ball
though apparently small and fragile could hit the
ball as far as the next man and was a really beautiful
putter, using an aluminium club and standing very
close to the ball with the heel of the club off the
ground. His actual stroke was hardly orthodox
according to all accepted teaching, for he swayed his
body perceptibly, but the sway was perfectly timed and
the whole movement graceful and rhythmic. I had
once asked John Ball, his namesake and presumably
some sort of distant relation, since both came from
Hoylake, what sort of golfer Tom Ball was. The
answer was 'I don't reckon him,' but for once the
great man was certainly too severe.

The irrepressible Duncan and Mayo again
challenged their elders, this time Braid and Taylor.
The match was played over Burhill, where Mayo
had become professional, and Walton Heath. The
seniors were five up at Burhill, and that was that;
they duly won by 8 and 7.

CHAPTER VIII

The End of a Golden Age, 1910-1914

As far as the *News of the World* was concerned 1910 was a still worse one than the year before for the veteran leaders. None of them was in the final at Sunningdale, which was fought out between Sherlock and Duncan, Sherlock winning. The Championship however only changed hands among the Triumvirate, James gaining his second victory at St. Andrews without any unhallowed dealings with the railway line. His finest round, I should imagine as fine a round as he ever played, was one that did not count. The ground was very hard, as it so often is at St. Andrews, so that if there comes a tremendous downpour of rain, there is always a danger of flooding. So it was this time; the water could not get away, the conditions became impossible and the day's play had to be abandoned. James had started some little while when the news reached him, but it may have come to him in so vague a form that he could not wholly trust it. In order to make quite sure he ploughed his way home through the floods and finished in 76. It was a sad waste, enough to have discouraged most men. However, when play began again next day it was in the very same score of 76 that he went round. It was a sound, steady start but it was three worse than that of the quicksilver Duncan and Duncan's 73 might have been even better, for this time it was he who fell foul of the railway at the

sixteenth. He played from it out on to the field
beyond and so back to the course but the hole cost
him 6.

In the afternoon Duncan took 77 and James over-
hauled him with a fine 73, beginning gloomily with
two 5's owing to bad putting, but being as near as
might be faultless afterwards. Braid led at 149 with
Duncan second at 150. At least so we all comfortably
thought. I remember the circumstances perfectly
because I had sent off my report, put on my dress
clothes and was finding my way out to dinner when
by Tom Morris's shop I became aware of a great
excitement and, a moment later, of a storm of applause
from the home green. Willie Smith of Mexico, one
of the great Carnoustie golfing family, returning after
years to the shores of his native land, had had the
audacity to go round in 71. It was, I think, a record
score and it certainly put him at the top of the list,
one stroke ahead of James. Here was a pretty state
of things for the poor reporter, due at a friend's table
in five minutes. I am glad to think that he took the
only manly course, let the figures speak for themselves
(that is always a useful phrase in such emergencies),
decided to tackle Mr. Smith next day and went
tranquilly to his dinner.

Of course a big crowd went out to see Willie Smith
next morning, but the putts were not flying in this
time and he was soon more or less out of the hunt.
It was Duncan who gave the pyrotechnic display with
another 71—36 out and 35 home. For sixteen holes
James's score was as good as Duncan's, but whereas
youth finished with a 4 and a 3, age took 6 at the
seventeenth, caused by a topped second and a weak
third into the Road bunker. So Duncan led with
221; Braid was 223, Herd 227 and Duncan went

out first. He started well enough but had 6's at the
fifth and sixth and fell to pieces. Once more the road
to victory was wide open for James and he was steady
as a rock. Four 4's made a heartening start : he took
three putts at the fifth and again at the seventh but
38 out was good enough and two 3's at the tenth and
eleventh, with the dreaded High Hole safely past,
made a triumphal procession of the rest of the round.
He went on perfectly 4, 4, 5, 4 and then, ending
rather lazily or rather cautiously, took three 5's for
another 38 and a 76, beating Herd by four shots.

It was the last of our Open Championships that he
was destined to win, though it would have been a
very rash prophet who foretold any such thing at the
time. He had won four in six years and five in ten
years, a unique achievement very unlikely to be
equalled, let alone surpassed. His winning score of
299 represented the first time that those proverbial
four 75's had been beaten round the Old Course.
If James could have known that this was to be his
last victory I think he would have liked it to be won
at St. Andrews and in his own Kingdom of Fife. As
far as other countries were concerned it was not his
last Championship, for this year he braved the chops
of the Channel once again and won the French Open
at La Boulie with a score of 298.

I said some time back that Jack White's Championship of 1904 at Sandwich was perhaps the most
exciting ever played but I made some tentative
claims for another Sandwich Championship, that of
1911. Now that I am coming to describe it I feel
those claims to be stronger than ever, but then I
must admit that I saw this one and did not see the
earlier one. At any rate this I can vouch for, that
there was never a Championship which made greater

demands for ubiquity on the wretched reporter. He often has to be in two or three places at once but this time he had to be at the very least in half a dozen, so many people were in the hunt almost up to the very last hole. Among these was certainly James, not perhaps in the very hottest of the hunt, since he never seemed quite to be winning, but as he only finished two shots behind the winner, Harry Vardon, he was emphatically to be reckoned with.

Vardon's health had this year greatly improved and he had besides gone in for a mild form of training, involving as much rest as possible, a light diet and severe restraint in the matter of tobacco. He was hitting the ball beautifully and putting more than respectably with his little Brown-Vardon putter with the small head and shallow face, at any rate till the last round. Then he did make a resolute effort to throw victory away and it was rather lucky for him that some of his most dangerous pursuers likewise faltered on the threshold. He got away to a good start with two thoroughly sound 74's but they did not give him the lead. Duncan, who had now taken to going up like the rocket and too often coming down like the stick, had begun with 73 and 71, four whole precious strokes better than Vardon, Taylor and Ray who came equal next. James together with Massy amongst others had tailed off a little with 151.

Next morning saw various chops and changes. The unfortunate Duncan had taken a fatal 83 as he had at St. Andrews the year before, while Vardon had gone serenely on his way with a 75. He had now a lead of three strokes at 223: Herd and Taylor were 226: Ray, Braid, Massy and Duncan 227: Harold Hilton, who was this year making a great come-back, 228. My memories are fragmentary in the extreme and I seemed to be continually watching one or other of the favourites play a hole or two and then taking the best shelter I could under a sandhill to write about them while the playful wind, quite a strong one, did its best to blow my papers away.

Vardon was out early and made his supporters terribly anxious. I think everyone was hoping that he would win after so long a time in the wilderness and it was dreadful to see him begin to drop the strokes especially on the greens. For once he had not gone home to rest and eat his light lunch at his hotel but ate a hearty meal at the club instead. Whether this had anything to do with it no one can say. At any rate he was round in 80 which was palpably not good enough, and at once there were half a dozen ravening wolves on his track.

The remarkable thing about this pursuit was not as in Jack White's year its splendid pertinacity but rather the way in which chances were thrown away. James doubtless had a good chance, since a 75 was very far from being beyond his powers, but somehow or other he was never quite doing it. The two real tragedies were those of Sandy Herd and Harold Hilton. Sandy arrived on the eighteenth tee wanting a 4 to win and a 5 to tie. He pulled his drive into the rough and took 6, a break-down all too like some of those of his earlier years. As to Hilton I can hardly bear to think of his last seven holes. I found him having just holed out on the ninth green where he had arrived completely unnoticed in 33, a score which threw him at a bound into the front rank with every chance of victory. I believe I was his sole spectator and he told me that it was an odd, disquieting sensation to be in a leading position again after so many years. He began home perfectly with two 4's and then

at the twelfth his tee shot, accurately placed as he
thought, was caught in an invisible corner of a bunker
which I have never passed since without cursing it in
my heart. It ought only to have cost him a stroke
but he missed a short putt and it did cost him two.
Moreover, it checked the flow of inspiration. Yet
even so he had the championship almost in the
hollow of his hand—thirteen strokes for the last three
holes to beat Vardon and one of those holes a short one.
Alas! he was bunkered at that short hole and took
5 and two more 5's completed the sad story. Taylor,
Ayton, Robson, Duncan, all had chances and had if
possible to be watched, and all took 78 or 79. And
then when Vardon's troubles seemed over at last, along
came Massy to play the last hole most beautifully in
4—two perfect wooden-club shots and two putts—
for a 76 and a tie.

The play-off of the tie was a great disappointment,
for while Vardon played lovely golf—I still think I
never saw better driving—Massy fell gradually behind
and finally picked up his ball on the thirty-fifth green.
I ought to have said that before the Championship
there was played a 'Coronation Match,' by thirty-six-
hole foursomes between the Professionals and
Amateurs, nine couples a side. One gallant pair of
Amateurs, Lionel Munn and Harold Beveridge, won
at the thirty-eighth hole. All the other Amateur
pairs were severely beaten. James played in the first
couple with Massy and they beat John Ball and
Chick Evans of America, who was what would today
be called a 'guest artist,' by 6 and 5.

It was in this year that there was for the first time, as
far as I know, a suggestion in the newspapers of James's
trouble with his eyes. They had bothered him
particularly in the earlier part of the season. At the

same time there was talk of his not putting so well as of old, complaints reminiscent of his first years in public, and probably the one trouble was partly due to the other. Nisbet's *Golf Year Book* tells me that in the *News of the World* tournament at Walton Heath he even forsook his old putter, 'to seek fresh inspiration and confidence in a new invention.' I saw that tournament and am the more ashamed that I had forgotten the fact and cannot now say what was the 'new invention'; it has some sound as of a patent. At any rate it enabled him to win for the fourth and, as it turned out, the last time, but only after two blood-curdling struggles. In the semi-final Tom Williamson of Hollinwell seemed to have him beaten, for he was two up with three to play. However Williamson, a little unluckily perhaps, lost the next two holes: the match was halved and James won far away from home at the twenty-second hole. He met Ray in the final and had him apparently at his mercy for he was six up with nine to play. Then began the process of the holes dropping away 'like snow off a dyke.' Ray, as far as I remember, holed some good putts and James made some slips—comparatively venial ones but they all counted; there never was a great spurt yet that did not get some encouragement from the other side. It seemed all over going to the seventeenth, but Ray scrambled gallantly out again and so James was dragged to the very last hole. It was the only time that, to my fancy, he looked a little anxious, for I had detected no visible anxiety after his 8 at Prestwick. At any rate he played the last hole without a quiver. There never was any doubt about his 4 but Ray's putt for a 3 stopped only a very little way short of the hole. It had been a 'close run thing.'

The gallant Ray never could quite win that tournament and in 1912 he was beaten in the final again,
and again by a single hole, this time by Harry Vardon,
who surprisingly enough had never won it before.
However Ray had ample compensation for he won
the Open Championship at Muirfield and won it
handsomely by four strokes and, what was more,
never looked likely to let anyone else win it.   He was
ostensibly a rough-hewn, unpolished, unorthodox
golfer but he had great strength and the invaluable
gift of rhythm, for all that he seemed to heave his
great body into the shot; he had too a pretty, delicate
touch round the green.   When he was in form he
looked intensely formidable and he was really in
form at Muirfield.   He jumped away at the start with
a 71 and added a 74 to it.   Harry Vardon came next
with 75 and 72 and then James a stroke behind at
148.   Muirfield had twice been a lucky course for
him and the superstitious among his admirers may
have positively rejoiced to see him start with a 77.
Was not that just how he had started in 1906 when
somebody else had started with 71, and yet had he not
won comfortably in the end?   Sure enough, James
pulled up with a splendid 71 in the second round, but
on the last day he was no more than moderate with
77 and 78 and there was no catching Ray with his 76
and 75.   Vardon made a gallant effort with a fourth
round of 71 but he had taken 81 in the morning.
Ray won with 295, Vardon took 299 and James was
303.
    One little scene from Ray's last round has stuck so
vividly in the mind that I must set it down.   It was at
the old fourteenth hole, a short hole across a big
cross-bunker, of no particular merit.   On the right
of the green there was a small pot bunker and as Ray

was about to play a knot of young professionals were standing in front of that bunker, thus masking it from the tee. John Ball, who was a steward, ran forward with his flag and insisted on their getting out of the way. They did so rather reluctantly and plump, down came Ray's ball in that very bunker. John came back with a light of malicious triumph in his eyes. The young men had looked pityingly at him as if to say 'We professionals don't put our pitches into bunkers.' Now perhaps they would know a little better another time.

1913, or at any rate the earlier part of the golfing season, was a bad year for James's eyes. He was advised not to play in the Open Championship. He disregarded the advice but he was a sad sight playing in dark glasses and from the start he was a long way down the list; the handicap was altogether too great. This is a book primarily about James, but sometimes his great contemporaries will come breaking in entirely on their own account when he is not much concerned, and it is impossible to pass over J. H.'s win at Hoylake, undoubtedly his greatest and perhaps anybody's greatest win anywhere. He began by saving his neck in the qualifying competition by holing a putt on the last green, five or six feet long—*horresco referens*—and that set him going in earnest. The weather on the first day was fine; perhaps the citizens of Hoylake who are very jealous about the weather would have called it a flat calm. It certainly was not that, but there was not much wind for Hoylake and Ray, the reigning Champion, playing very finely, led with 73 and 74; J. H. was one behind him with 73 and 75.

And then in the night the wind, of which Hoylake boasts so arrogantly, awoke and showed what it really could do. The Exhibition tents were prone on the ground, a mass of tangled ropes and flapping canvas, and the rain swept ever and anon across the links in bitter squalls. I have woken up to two other terrible mornings in Championship weeks, those of Cotton's Championship at Carnoustie in 1937 and Reg Whitcombe's at Sandwich in the following year, but 1913 was, I think, worse than either of them. It was hard to walk against the wind without turning tail now and then for a rest, and as to hitting against it—well, I take two eloquent statements from J. H.'s autobiography. The first hole at Hoylake that bends its way round that dreadful field of out-of-bounds memories is said in the books to measure 435 yards in length. It took J. H. two full shots with wood to reach the corner of the field, then another wooden club shot and a long run-up put him near the hole and down went the putt for 5. Poor light-weight Michael Moran who had been on his heels the day before began with a 10. The third hole is longer, 480 yards: it took J. H. three full shots, a sixty-yard run-up and a putt for another 5. He went round in 77 and if ever there was a better round played in a tempest I have never heard of it. In the afternoon, when the wind had ever so slightly abated he had a 79, containing his tremendous 3 at the Briars, where his driving-mashie shot nearly knocked the pin out of the hole and he lay dead for a 3. He won with 304 against Ray's 312, and the glory of the Briars still dazzles my sight.

James's eyes were obviously better in the autumn, for with the *News of the World* played at Walton Heath he reached the final again, but lost to George Duncan by 3 and 2. I had just landed from America where I had seen Francis Ouimet, hardly more than a schoolboy, achieve his memorable defeat of Vardon and Ray in the American Open Championship at The Country Club at Brookline. And now on the top of that iconoclastic feat the very first news that I had heard on getting home was that Duncan, not so young as Francis by any means, but yet of the younger generation, had had the audacity to beat James standing at bay in his own stronghold. Here, I felt with Sir Leicester Dedlock, were 'the obliteration of landmarks, the opening of floodgates and the uprooting of distinctions.' What was the world coming to?

The golfing world seemed once more stabilized in 1914, with Vardon and Taylor fighting out a tremendous battle at Prestwick for the Open Championship and Francis Ouimet, who had gallantly invaded us, a long way down the list. He has often shown us his real game since then, but the first visit, as has often been the case with others, was something too much for him. All three members of the Triumvirate had now won five Championships and each was eager to take the lead. If they had known the future it was their last chance. By 1920 James and Vardon would be fifty years old and Taylor forty-nine. There could have been no more perfectly exciting start, for after the first round Vardon was at the top of the tree with 73 followed by the other two with 74 apiece. In the second round James began to let the putts slip— the greens were terrifying in their keenness—and 82 put him as near as might be out of the hunt. The next day it was all Vardon and Taylor. The malignant goddess who rules over the draw had seen to it that their names came out of the hat together; and that at Prestwick of all places where the crowds were always large and impatient of discipline and the conformation of the course with its famous loop of the last four holes made the controlling of them a really desperate task.

James was out of the hunt and yet he may be said to have had something to do with the destination of that Championship. At any rate his old friend Taylor thought so. He had been consulted about new bunkers for the course and amongst others he had placed one on the way to the fourth hole, tempting the player narrowly to skirt the Pow Burn on the right. Vardon had led by two shots at the end of two rounds, but a magnificent, fighting 74 by Taylor had reversed the position after the third round. Now Taylor led by two strokes and he still held that lead going to the fateful fourth. Vardon with the honour pulled his tee shot safely away to the left but Taylor went for the gap between the new bunker and the burn and was caught in the sand by the burn side. It was not a bad place: he might often have put the ball close to or on to the green but this time he fluffed it sadly into the burn and the hole cost him 7. That decided the Championship: Vardon won by three strokes and J. H. declared that James ought to be buried in his own bunker with a niblick through his heart. And after that came the war; there was no *News of the World* and no more championships till 1920. The long, golden afternoon was over.

CHAPTER IX

Sundown

THE coming of war in 1914 naturally and profoundly affected golf all over the country. It is difficult to remember exactly in looking back but I incline to think that this was even more notable in the first war than it was in the second. It was such a long time since there had been a war in Europe that its coming seemed to mean a more complete disturbance and uprooting of ordinary life. Of course, golf was played to some extent and as in the second war the leading professionals gave their services freely for various war charities. The Triumvirate and Herd, all well over military age—James was now forty-four —travelled up and down the country playing exhibition matches in the good cause. They did other war tasks as well. James used to go over to Tattenham Corner on munition work and in addition he and three other friends cultivated a large field of potatoes. His son Harry, then a schoolboy, remembers him getting up regularly at six o'clock in the morning to this end. It was incidentally during this first war, in December 1916, that James was reported in the papers to have been killed in an accident at Waterloo Station. An unfortunate gentleman, Mr. James A. Braid of Southsea, had slipped in running for a train and had died. He had apparently some claims to be regarded as a golfer and hence the mistake. The first news of it to reach J. H. Taylor was a request for a column of appreciation of his old friend: luckily he was soon undeceived, but some notices were, I believe, published before the mistake was discovered. James was thus one of the very few people who have had the good or bad fortune to read their own obituaries. It was an experience which he would have endured with complete philosophy, and it was mercifully thirty-four years before that column was wanted.

Perhaps though it is out of chronological order I may here interpolate a word or two as to the second war. When this war came James was hard on seventy. He was too old for war work and carried on with his job at Walton Heath, feeling now particularly responsible for the course. He took part in one or two exhibition matches in the early months of the war, which were extremely entertaining, since they brought back the gutty ball. It was not now however the champions of the past who played with the old friend on which they had been brought up. They were given the rubber-core to help them along against lusty youth, who must use the stony-hearted gutty. It made a thoroughly interesting game and, as far as I remember, there was very little in it in point of length, the flexibility of rubber more or less exactly compensating for the stiffness of old bones. I saw two of these foursomes, one at Sandy Lodge and one at Mid-Surrey. Cotton and Compston, if I remember rightly, represented youth. James played twice on the side of age, at Sandy Lodge with Havers as his partner and at Mid-Surrey, as was only proper, with J. H. Taylor. Both matches were halved, than which there could have been no better ending. I can still see clearly the scene on the last green at Sandy Lodge: James just settling down to tackle a putt of perhaps a good long yard for a half and Cotton coming up and with a very pretty gesture knocking the ball away. The Mid-Surrey match was a dramatic one. Cotton and Compston with their gutty played the most perfect imaginable golf to the turn which they reached, I think, in 36. They were then four up and the venerable and illustrious seemed beyond hope. However youth began to get involved in trees while age took noble advantage of its chances. In the end Fortune's wheel had taken so complete a turn that J. H. was left with a putt of no extraordinary length to win the match on the last green—a 'nasty' one no doubt but not a long one. He failed and James who was standing by me whispered, 'I never thought he'd miss that one.' The implied compliment was great, and indeed no man in the world was less likely to miss a putt when, having once been down, he now had his enemy at his mercy. However, miss it he did and perhaps it was all for the best.

I have deliberately broken the sequence of my story to get the odious subject of war as far as possible out of the way once and for all. Now let me get back to things in their right order and to the year 1919. When at last the war was over golf took some time to get back into its stride. With all the younger men on the green staff serving, the courses naturally fell into considerable disrepair. On the whole, considering all things, they had suffered very little and much hard work was put in by older members of the clubs who banded themselves together to look after particular putting greens. Still it was inevitable that the jungle tide of the rough should encroach on the fairway, that the heather should grow ever fiercer and more tangled, that the greens should grow smaller. And of course the standard of play was for some while far below what it had been in the summer

of 1914. No one can play little or no golf for four or
five years and hope instantly to begin again where he
left off. His swing may look as good as ever it was
but for the moment he has inevitably lost much of the
old accuracy of striking. His mind moreover has been
on other things; he has forgotten many of the tips
and dodges that were so familiar and the old feel of
the shot that he knew so intimately though he could
not perhaps put it into words. Enthusiasm may come
back with a rush but concentration will lag behind.
It was such good fun to be playing golf again that for
a while it was difficult to take the game with sufficient
earnestness.

Six years without a Championship was a long gap
for the youngest and a terribly long one for James
and his contemporaries. They had been forty-three
and forty-four when golf had come to a full stop
and, humanly speaking, had another Championship
or two in them before the years began to tell. Now,
when golf had come gradually to life again—and there
were no Championships in 1919, the first summer of
peace—they were hovering on fifty and that was a
very different affair. They were still likely to play
one or two rounds as well as ever but four rounds on
the top of a qualifying competition—there was the
rub. On the whole I should say that most people
fancied that their sun was set. I remember being
goaded, by what I thought excessive language, into
making a bet that no one of the Triumvirate would
win another Championship. I felt rather heartless
and disloyal and ashamed and am glad to remember
that I was never paid. It would have seemed like
blood money.

There was not much opportunity in 1919 for
judging whether these views were sound or otherwise.

There was one competition on the lines of the Open Championship and generally called the 'Unofficial' Championship, played at St. Andrews. It ended in a tie between George Duncan and Abe Mitchell and so confirmed the belief that these were the two heirs presumptive to the crown. The *News of the World* tournament was duly revived in the autumn at Walton Heath, when Duncan and Mitchell met in the final and Mitchell won. These two seemed at that moment destined fully to occupy the places of the great ones of the past, and then in 1920 came the first post-war Championship, at Deal, in which they were the most dramatic figures. It is true that they did not finish first and second; Duncan through his glorious golf on the last day won, but Mitchell, who had seemed to have the prize in his grasp, could never recover from his tragic start in the third round and finished fourth. Youth, if it may so be termed, for Duncan was now six and thirty, was served at last, but age made a wonderful and gallant fight of it; not this time in the form of the Triumvirate but that of their senior, Sandy Herd. He finished in 305, two strokes behind the winner and in his fourth round he had a fatal 7 at the sixteenth hole. It was a harrowingly, heartbreakingly near thing.

Taylor was twelfth with 316, Vardon two places behind him with 318 and James two strokes behind Vardon with 320. His four rounds were 79, 80, 79, 82, steady enough but lacking the old spark of divine fire. The old ones were far from done with yet; there were one or two more great days coming but the greatest were over. Later in the summer the *News of the World* was played at Mid-Surrey and Mitchell won again, beating Joshua Taylor, J. H.'s brother, in the final. None of the Quarte Major was in the last four. The sceptre of supreme dominion had definitely passed into other hands. But the two who seemed clearly marked out to hold it, though they had the skill and the power, had not quite the dogged-ness or the tenacity of those whom they had succeeded. They had not, I think, quite the same love of the fight; they were not always in the mood whereas the great ones of the past had by sheer strength of character forced themselves into the mood.

It must be always a little sad for an old Champion however modest, and however resigned to the in-evitable, to see the crowds that once attended him, now watching another. We in this country are wonderfully loyal to the great game-players of the past, but even so if we look with sad, faithful eyes on the setting sun, we hail with excited shouts the rising one. So in those first Championships after the war it was Duncan and Mitchell who took away the big crowds, leaving the elder heroes to those who loved their beautiful art for its own sake and never gave up hope that they would arise in their might and sweep intrusive youth from the field.

It was not only our own younger generations that had at last successfully challenged those who had kept them in subjection so long. The invaders from America became suddenly menacing and took away the crowds with them. In 1920 at Deal there were Jim Barnes, a Cornishman and still a British subject but an American golfer by adoption, and Walter Hagen, the first of the great American 'homebreds.' Barnes finished sixth, six strokes behind Duncan and Hagen finished something like sixtieth, without a soul to look at him, but showing a gallant and un-flagging spirit. Then in 1921 at St. Andrews and for the first time we realized, though even then not fully, the imminence and greatness of the peril. Jock Hutchison tied with Roger Wethered and won the play-off. Kerrigan, another American, was third, Hagen was creeping up the list and he and Barnes tied at 302, six shots behind the leaders. Melhorn and French were further away, not seriously to be considered at the moment, but it was clear that we should now be subjected to a regular and ever more formidable assault from over the sea. We would have given much to put back the clock and have our old stalwarts to resist it. Once again the eldest of them all, Herd, made a great effort. With one round to go he led Hutchison by four strokes and had gone round with superb consistency in 75, 74, 73. Alas! he took 80 for the last round against Hutchison's 70. James, four strokes worse than Herd, was admirably steady, 75, 77, 76, 78, but he was no longer capable apparently of quite the old sparkle. Taylor finished like a lion on the last day with 75 and 74, but a second round of 88 had inevitably destroyed him. Vardon too finished with a 74, one ahead of him.

It is pleasant to record that in this year the Triumvirate played their part and that successfully in the first international match between the professionals of Britain and America. Before the Championship a match was played at Gleneagles. This was six years before the institution of the Ryder Cup; the American team was not one chosen for the match but consisted of those who had come over to play in the Championship, while the British team, though a good one, seems to have had one or two gaps. If, however, it was not an intensely solemn match over two days and seventy-two holes, it was a perfectly serious one and we were glad to win it, if not so humbly glad as we should have been a few years later. James played with his old partner J. H.—they were the third couple out of five—and halved with Fred McLeod, a returned Scotsman, and Clarence Hackney. In the singles James playing at number six beat Hackney 5 and 4. Britain won the day by nine matches to three with three halved. The next such match was not played till 1926, at Wentworth, and then for our ageing heroes it was too late.

Next year, 1922 at Sandwich, with three American players in the first four and one of them Hagen, the winner, it was Taylor's turn to uphold the honour of age with a very fine score of 304, only four behind the winner with Vardon four behind him again. Neither Herd nor Braid were this time in the picture and next year at Troon Herd's was the only name among the first thirty-six and that was rather far down. Youth in the shape of Arthur Havers had come gloriously to the rescue of Britain and nothing else seemed greatly to matter. We rashly assumed that the rot had been stopped once and for all. In fact we were on the brink of long-enduring disaster. Havers was destined to be the last Briton to win for eleven years.

However it is not my purpose to tell the story of American victories but to look at the 'sundown splendid and serene' of James and the elder brethren. At Hoylake in 1924, with the course more than ever formidable from a sudden and monstrous growth of long grass that had almost beaten the greenkeepers, James began with two 80's and ended better with 78 and 76. Herd beat him by four shots and Vardon's name does not appear, but Taylor was the uncrowned king of the Championship. He finished fifth in his fifty-fourth year, and if the scores in the two qualifying rounds could have been counted he would actually have been first. I mention this as a point of academic interest. Of course, and this is a point that ecstatic persons do not always appreciate, the frame of mind in which qualifying rounds are played and the strain involved are entirely different in kind from those in the Championship itself. If they counted toward the ultimate total they would not be qualifying rounds; the whole mental outlook of the players and so the whole play would be different. But it is truly remarkable that a man of fifty-three can complete six rounds, whatever the circumstances, in a lower score than anyone else in a championship field. I incline to think that this was the 'finest hour' of this great warrior.

In 1925 at Prestwick, Jim Barnes's year, Taylor again led the old brigade, ten strokes behind the winner with 310. Herd was 314 and Vardon 315 and I can find no trace of James in the first forty. Eyesight and, in consequence, putting is, I think, a reasonable explanation so far as any is needed beyond the gliding of the years. But in the next year at St. Anne's, Bobby Jones's first year, he springs up again with 311, an 82 which was a millstone, then two 75's and a respectable 79 to end with. Good enough in all conscience at fifty-six years old, one would think, but not good enough to catch either Taylor or Herd. J. H. finished eleventh and his best round of 71 was better than any of Bobby's four; Herd was four shots worse than J. H. And then came J. H.'s last year at St. Andrews, and James managed to beat his old friend, something that he had not done since the war. He had four wonderfully steady rounds, 75, 77, 76 and 78, and beat J. H. by five strokes; but he could not beat Herd who ended with a 71, a really tremendous display of fireworks, and a total of 300. The thought of these glorious old gentlemen stirs the blood.

One round, or even two, perhaps, but an average of
75 for four rounds at St. Andrews, that is heroic work
and Sandy was born in 1868. Take 1868 from 1927
and there is very little change left out of sixty.

Yes, they were wonderful, and I must leave the
Championship for a moment and turn back to the
News of the World in 1926. It was played at Mid-
Surrey and Herd won it, beating Bloxham in the final
at the thirty-eighth hole. The weather, as I remember
it, had been fine and hot for some time and the
ground was full of running, doubtless a help to the
venerable. It suited Herd who made skilful use of
his hook. I can see him now drawing the right foot
ever a little further back as he waggled, till at length
he felt himself ready to let fly. Bloxham's arrival in
the final was frankly a great surprise, for he was not
very young nor very long and he was hampered by
lameness, but he played with great steadiness and re-
solution and putted splendidly. Herd could not get
away from him, and then as they set out to play the
extra holes there came suddenly a drenching deluge of
rain. But it was the old gentleman that weathered
the storm best and he won at the second hole.

That was glorious and it seemed next year at Walton
Heath that the glory might be repeated for James
reached the final and there were visions of such
rejoicings as the heath had never seen before. It
turned out a sad day. For some reason that I do not
now remember, I had not seen the earlier play;
James in the final had come with a shock of surprise
and joy and I had started out on the drive from Kent
into Surrey full of hope and excitement that even the
ceaseless rain could not damp. But it rained and it
rained and it kept on raining. Compston who was
James's conqueror played very fine golf and was a

deserving winner beyond all question, but it was no day for a man of seven and fifty, at the end of several rounds of hard fighting. Moreover before the match started James, as was his conscientious habit on these big occasions, had already been out to see that all was well with the course. It was, as Mr. Tony Weller would have said, 'unekal.' Compston won a good long way from home, about the twelfth hole I think, in the afternoon, and it was a sad procession of damp and depressed patriots that splashed its long way back to the club. Our hopes had been so high and so much the more bitter the disappointment. Metaphorically we had seen the rockets poised ready on their sticks and heard the band playing 'See the Conquering Hero.' We had too truculently defied the years and they had had their revenge. James alone remained perfectly tranquil: he had fought the good fight and, as far as the great events were concerned, he had finished his course.

That last statement is perhaps a little too rhetorical, for James's name appears again in the Championship at Sandwich in 1928 and indeed, though that is the last time it is recorded among those who qualified and returned four scores, he persisted for some years with a very placid philosophy. Taylor, who had lasted the best of the Triumvirate, was the first to hang up his arms. He did so, I fancy, not unthankfully. As long as there was even the faintest hope he could and would fight on with unabated vigour, but once there was none it was time to stop and to be frankly happy in looking on. The others could presumably enjoy playing without seriously competing: to play was part of the festival and so they went on. It was entirely a matter of temperament and each was right to take his own way. In this year of 1928 at Sandwich, the last of James's Championships to be here recorded, he had a total of 316—one better than Harry Vardon—80, 79, 81, 76. So it will be seen that he finished with a really good round. One who saw some of it tells me that James played beautifully accurate golf and had quite a gallery, largely of his brother professionals to greet him with respectful applause as he walked off the last green. It was thirty-three years since he had played on the same course in his first Open Championship.

CHAPTER X

Life at Walton Heath

ALL this time I have been following James's Championship career and have said nothing of his everyday life at Walton Heath. He was naturally a good deal away from Walton in the full tide of the golfing season, though not to quite the same extent, I think, as a professional in a corresponding position is away from his home club today. There was not then that constant round of tournaments that has turned the leading professionals into a travelling circus. The Triumvirate and one or two others undoubtedly played a number of exhibition matches; they had not merely the cream of that business but had in effect all of it. They travelled enough for James with his astonishingly accurate memory to obtain a knowledge of trains, connections and junctions that was 'extensive and peculiar.' Robert McKenzie, whom I have already quoted as one of his earliest assistants, says that there seemed to be hardly a considerable station in England or Scotland where James was not hailed by some friend at court, guard or ticket-collector or station-master. So in these busy times the leading players were here, there and everywhere for short spells, staying in one place perhaps only for a single night. Taylor wanted to read his newspaper and the others wanted to play penny nap and J. H. reluctantly gave in to the majority. No doubt it was hard, harassing work and it was wonderful that they maintained so consistently high a standard. In the winter they enjoyed compara- tive tranquillity, as far as public engagements were concerned, and it is of James's life in the winter that I am now thinking, because it was then that I used to see him at Walton and sometimes play with him.

It must have been, as far as I can now tell, about 1908, after I had abandoned the Temple and sold my eloquently clean wig, that I began to go with some regularity to Walton Heath. Lord Riddell—he had not yet become Lord—was by this time a person of great authority, indeed of supreme authority, at Walton and he used to call for me in his big open car, which whirled us to Walton, a journey so icy that I had to buy a special greatcoat in which to endure it. We would then perhaps play a foursome with James and somebody else. On several occasions, I re- member, it was Dr. W. G. Grace. To travel with him in a car gave the sensation of a royal progress, since that vast beard, by then 'a sable silvered,' seemed to be recognized by the passers-by even at the most fleeting glance. On the course moreover there could never be any doubt as to his presence, so cheerful and emphatic was his greeting of any passing friend, divided from him by the extent of a fairway or two. In *Advanced Golf* James took W. G. to point his moral in writing of the cricket stroke at golf. 'I have,' he says, 'watched the strokes being made by many prominent cricketers, including Dr. W. G. Grace who plays a fair amount of golf now, and from what I have seen I am convinced that the length he gets is the result of muscular force pure and simple, together with very pronounced and strong wrist action, which amounts to much the same thing. The amount of wrist-work that Dr. Grace gets into his tee shots is quite remarkable.' I may humbly add on my own account that the Doctor's driving, absolutely fast-footed, was uncommonly straight, but the iron clubs proved too much even for his genius; his favourite iron club which he called his 'cleaver' was not to be relied on.

Lord Riddell wasted no time; the moment we reached the club the bowler hat which he invariably wore in the car was exchanged for a cap, James was ready in the shop and off we went. Similarly when the day's golf was over the bowler was instantly reassumed and in less than no time we were being frozen on Banstead Downs. He was a remarkable golfer in that he was inclined to talk continuously on all sorts of subjects during the round and yet keep his mind on the match which he very properly liked to win. He had, I think, the gift which one or two famous American golfers, notably Walter Hagen, have possessed, of 'letting up' between strokes and then on the instant concentrating fiercely. He was likewise a remarkable golfer in that he played tolerably well, to a handicap of eight or nine as I remember, in a method that looked at first sight wholly prohibitive of success. He was not by nature a game-player, having had little time in youth for such things, but he was an intensely resolute man and I think he and James between them had made the very best of unpromising material. I have in my mind a vivid picture of him putting with his right foot drawn far back, while he leered or perhaps I should say scowled at the ball over his left shoulder. It looked uncomfortable but he was a good holer of a nasty putt at a pinch. That was one of his merits as a foursome player, and another was that, at any rate with James

as his partner, he was unexpectedly docile and sub-
mitted himself to his superior's advice, never playing
what an old Scottish caddie once called 'a proud
game.' I think it was also due directly or indirectly
to Lord Riddell that Walton Heath had a decidedly
political atmosphere. Eminent statesmen and newspaper editors and proprietors were often to be seen
there and they may even have said more or less un-
guarded things, knowing that by the discreet James
they would never be repeated. In these circles I
never moved but I fancy the politicians were chiefly
but not wholly of the Liberal persuasion. Lloyd
George, Winston Churchill, Masterman, Arthur
Balfour—here are some distinguished names from that
now apparently remote past to which Sir Frederick
Hamilton referred in his speech at the dinner to
James celebrating his eightieth birthday, which I
quote later. Mr. Churchill is said to have declared
that golf 'seemed a good game for conversation.'
James, and this is a point mentioned by Sir Frederick
Hamilton, apparently regarded Mr. Churchill as the
inventor of the form of golf called a 'greensome.'
That is, perhaps I had better explain, as defined in
The Golfer's Handbook, 'a species of four-ball competition. Both players in a combination play tee shots,
and afterwards continue with one of the balls which
is nominated.' With partners of much the same
handicap the longer tee shot is generally chosen,
provided the lie be good, but with partners of such
unequal merits as a Cabinet Minister and an Open
Champion, other and subtler considerations may
decide the choice. More or less exhaustive researches
have so far failed to confirm the attribution of this
game to so distinguished a source, but no doubt he
may have been the first to introduce it to James's

notice. I may add that whoever else did invent it, his name, like that of the last Laird of Ravenswood, is 'lost for evermo'.'

What happened in such foursomes as I played I have no recollection nor would it be of any interest if I had, but I recall very clearly what pains James invariably took over his play, studying his putts as if the fate of empires depended on them and never allowing himself even the suspicion of a slack or hasty shot. I used to think at the time that this was part of a deliberate system, adopted because he felt it dangerous to lapse even for a moment into anything like carelessness. No doubt also he conscientiously felt that he must give nothing under his best to those who took him out to play with them. But I feel now that there was one supreme reason, the simplest of all, for this high standard of care, namely that he loved playing golf so much for its own sake, that no matter how unimportant the match, it would never enter his head not to try his hardest. He always tried to play his best and he never showed by word or gesture the faintest sign of disappointment if he did not. Perfect golfing manners could not further go. Among the letters received by his sons after his death I choose one on this particular point. 'Of my memories of your father,' a friend wrote, 'one is outstanding. About thirty years ago I played round Walton Heath with him. Just what was wrong I never learned but he took nearer 90 than 80 to go round and that when he was not far past his best. On the way round he never made a single reference to his game and produced no alibi or excuse, but chatted of other things as usual. At the end he just said, "I didn't give you a very good game." It was the greatest lesson on how golf should be played I ever had in my life.'

James was of course an ideal foursome partner for any erratic player on account of his powers of recovery. The thickest heather parted before his stupendous blow. It is true that there were spots on Walton Heath that defied even him. I remember in 1937 watching the match between Cotton and Densmore Shute. At the fourteenth hole, as the course then was, Shute pulled his tee shot into a really dreadful place in the heather, and James with an almost malignant, not to say un-christian, smile murmured, 'He'll want all his dynamiters there.' Apropos of James and the heather I must allow myself one pleasant little story, even though it be rather old. A shining light of musical comedy was one day brought down by an admiring friend and she was given James as her partner. Hole after hole she toppled her ball gently into the heather and James retrieved it with a mighty heave. But at last there came a lie, in which a young fir tree played its part. James removed some of the tree but the ball remained more or less where it was. Then with her most radiant smile the lady remarked, 'I am so glad to see even you can sometimes make a mistake, Mr. Braid.'

There never could be a more encouraging partner nor one whose perfect placidity communicated itself as far as possible to those less tranquil in temperament. He was paternally kind and while saying hardly a word he could yet spread a soothing and healing balm around him. A little example of this kindness, though this was not in a foursome, was given me by a friend the other day. He only played with James once, when he went down as a stranger to Walton and finding the great man disengaged asked him for a game. After some holes James told him that he did not know how to get out of bunkers. 'There's nobody behind,' he said, 'and plenty of time,' and forthwith threw a number of balls down into a bunker and superintended the process of reformation. It was a small thing perhaps but not many people would have so gone out of their way; at any rate the beneficiary has never forgotten it.

This I fear is a rather desultory chapter but one more foursome comes into my head showing how well James knew the game of those with whom he played regularly at Walton. James's partner was Mr. Stephen Winkworth, not a great player by any means save in one respect, but a formidable opponent in any kind of money match and in particular a really great putter in a method of his own. He stood facing the hole with the ball between his feet and putted it back-handed with his left hand. At the shorter putts he was deadly and James used to say that he was the best holer-out he had ever seen. Who was my partner I have forgotten but I remember that it was a very foggy day and that on the New Course, then one of nine holes, he and I were at some disadvantage in not knowing where we were and what club to take. We therefore clung as closely as was decent to our adversaries, hoping to glean some hints from James's directions to his partner. Here we were disappointed for they appeared to have a secret code, as have, I understand, American football players. 'Forgan, sir,' was a most delusive piece of advice as far as we were concerned. Next came a 'full pipe' and later again after some consultation it was decided that a 'half Simpson' would be sufficient. However I am glad to say that this time they were wrong for the ball was bunkered and a full Simpson would have been better. Finally a club called 'Snakes' laid a long and serpentine run-up stone dead, the flag being wholly out of sight. The key to the code is simple enough. Forgan and Simpson naturally refer to those famous club-makers. A pipe is the mark employed by the equally famous Mr. Stewart of St. Andrews and a snake decorated the clubs made for ladies by some illustrious forger of heads, I think Mr. Stewart again. Our eavesdropping was of very little service to us.

Day after day people wanted to play with James and he was ready and willing to play with them. I had a notion that he laid down for himself one rule of abstinence, namely never to play more than two rounds a day, but I am told that I was wrong and that he certainly did on occasions play three. In *Advanced Golf* he refers to the third round as an occasionally pardonable indulgence to be generally avoided. Moreover he played in all sorts of weather and Walton can be as bleak a spot as need be. No wonder he was one of the pioneers in the matter of mackintosh trousers. Gloves he ever scorned but he may now and then have condescended to the comforting muffetee. How he avoided growing stale I cannot imagine, but he was very strong, he liked playing golf much better than doing anything else and acquired, I suppose, a sort of permanent second wind. There is a story of someone asking him what form of training he adopted. 'What for?' he asked. 'Why, to keep fit.' 'I'm aye fit,' was the answer and that disposed of the question.

He must in fact have been wonderfully fit, for his son Harry tells me he never recalls him having a day in bed nor a day off of any kind except once or twice when his eyes were at their worst. The only holidays he took were golfing ones. In the summer when his two boys were small he would take them and their

mother up to stay with the grandparents at Earlsferry but he did not stay there long himself; he was
generally summoned to go on some golfing holiday
with one of the members of Walton Heath. I
remember to have spent a few days in his company
on one such excursion when Lord Riddell had taken
a pleasant house at Gullane. James was full of
holiday enthusiasm. He would, I am sure, have
played three rounds every day if any other member
of the party had felt equal to it. It was on this occasion
that there occurred a little incident which was
recorded by another of my fellow-guests, Arthur
Croome. As I happened to be there and as it shows
how even the greatest of men can blandly commit
the most outrageous crimes, I will set it down. It
appears that Croome had more or less overtly stolen
from John Low a certain straight-faced iron of
precious quality, in exchange for a putting-cleek which
John had previously stolen from him. The story now
goes on as Croome told it in the *Morning Post*: 'Some
twelve months later James Braid and I were both
staying in a hospitable house at Gullane. On the
afternoon of his last day we played on opposite sides
in a four ball match at Hedderwick, a charming
private course which was ploughed up during the
war. I went out in 32 and my side turned six down.
Braid's score at that point was 28 and his partner
had come in twice. Braid completed the round in
57. Before we went out Braid had taken my John
Low iron and waggled it appreciatively. In the
course of his round he borrowed it, I think, twice, to
lay a long second stone dead. After dinner that
evening, he took me aside and told me he thought it
would be a pity if that club should be denied opportunity to contribute to the winning of a championship

or two. I said rather grudgingly but at the same time more than half pleased: "Oh, all right; I suppose you've got to have it! I'll go and fetch it for you." "You needn't trouble," replied James, "it's in my bag. I just thought I would tell you about it!"'

As far as I know James permitted himself only one self-denying ordinance as to golf. He would never give a lesson on a Sunday. Whether this was the surviving effect of his early bringing-up I do not know. At any rate, though he played on Sunday he never taught. Otherwise and on all the other days of the week he gave plenty of lessons, so that there were very few crannies of his time unfilled. If there were any and things were busy in the shop, he would now and then take his coat off and lend a hand there. There were good clubs made in that shop, but it was chiefly for his own clientele among his own members. Neither did he make any great feature of the shop; here was no glittering show of the various things that today go to make up golfing 'equipment'; his bill-heads remained always the same modest documents; by comparison with his successors he stood fast in the old ways. As a teacher he was, I believe, excellent. I cannot speak from personal experience since I had but one lesson from him and that a casual one, for which he resolutely refused to be paid. It struck me then that he had laid a penetrating finger on some of my many weaknesses, of which I had been dimly aware myself. He soon had me hitting the ball in a most satisfactory manner and though I relapsed afterwards I have never forgotten, though I may not have observed, his wise commandments.

Among his keenest pupils at one time was the Duke of Windsor, when Prince of Wales. Among James's papers after his death was found preserved a little note in pencil from the Prince enclosing a score-card, as a pupil's testimony to the master's teaching. This score ought to have been under 80 but a good second to the last hole had pitched in the rough a few inches over the green and so the triumph had not been achieved. 'I only wish,' the note ended, 'you had been playing round with me.'

His doctrine was not, I think, an elaborate one, nothing comparable in complexity indeed to what is sometimes preached nowadays, and it was probably none the worse for that. I find it hard to believe that the average Saturday afternoon golfer can usefully absorb a fraction of the instruction, couched in highly technical language, that is poured out for his supposed benefit. Some of the older teaching was fourth-form stuff by comparison with the sixth-form lessons that are now presumed to be intelligible to people with double-figure handicaps; and again I think that it was none the worse and perhaps much the better for that. It is true that photography has been of great help, alike in establishing facts as to what the best players actually do and in dispelling illusions as to what they thought they did. Certain standards of truth have therefore been arrived at and the modern teacher to some extent begins where his predecessors left off. Even so, being a conservative person I incline to hold that he is often too subtle and that the teacher of an older and simpler fashion, such as James was, might have an effect at once more calming and more beneficial. That he had a wonderfully shrewd and observant eye I have no doubt at all. He probably never put into words all he knew about the game but what he did say was most valuable.

To me *Advanced Golf* always seems to contain a great deal of eminently sound teaching on golf. Of course it was not written with his own hand but was talked to a reasonably enfranchised interpreter, and that does not make the teacher's task any easier. It is not an exciting book; it does not profess to have discovered the one secret of hitting the ball; James was far too honest and too calm a man for any such antics. Consequently the book is not one of those that cause the enthusiastic reader to leap to his feet and execute a practice swing with the poker while shouting 'Eureka!' But it is above everything a sensible book, just as its author was a sensible man. After James's death a cousin, writing to one of his sons, mentioned their last journey together. 'In the course of our journey,' he wrote, 'when we had the compartment to ourselves, I took advantage of his expert knowledge to say to him that I could usually manage to hit my drives fairly straight but that I felt I ought to get a greater length and enquired what I should do about it. His only comment was "Be content!"' How much sense is compressed into those two words! There is a story recounted of James for which I refuse to vouch; indeed I gravely doubt its truth. It is said that a stranger came down to play a game with the sage of Walton and it was arranged that he should receive the odds of a half. On the way to the tee he said that he had just read *Advanced Golf* and had high hopes accordingly. 'In that case,' the author replied, 'I will give you two-thirds.' As I say, I regretfully disbelieve the story, but assuming that golfing literature has any such immediately baleful effect, then I think that *Advanced Golf* would do the reader less harm that any other I know.

If he had done the writing of it himself unaided,

the book would have been characterized by his habitual economy of words. As it is, it seems at times unduly expanded. The interpreter too missed the little spirt of humour which must have crept in ever and anon. So the book is a serious, sometimes almost a laborious one, but it contains much sound and helpful advice and, here and there, some capital little tips, if that word may be respectfully used. It is interesting to find James true to his early bringing-up and particularly to St. Andrews, so full of admiration for the run-up shot and so eager for his pupils to learn it. Likewise his advice on putting, as being that of a converted sinner who has seen the light, is full of good, plain sense. I was once asked to advise as to a golfer who had flown too enthusiastically from one professional teacher to another until he had bemused and bemoidered his brain. I suggested that he go instantly to Walton Heath where he would find a physician to exert at once a sedative and a simplifying influence, and I am glad to say that for some time at least the result was most gratifying. James, I believe, enjoyed teaching as he enjoyed everything else to do with golf, and that was part but by no means all of his secret as a teacher.

I take it that James's most distinguished pupil as a player was beyond doubt Sir Ernest Holderness, one of the very best of all amateur golfers. But having written that sentence I am not sure whether 'pupil' is exactly the right word. When Sir Ernest as a young man first came to live at Walton he played a great deal with James and that was in itself an education; but he tells me that the master did not coach him much or at all in the ordinary sense of the word. Doubtless he realized that here was a player who did not want teaching, since he did things in the right way both by instinct and his own intelligence and so was best left alone. That Sir Ernest greatly profited by those games he has always been eager to acknowledge. Perhaps in the language of *Kim* I should call him James's 'Chelah.' Under whatever description it was a very happy association.

CHAPTER XI

Golf Architecture

WE have seen James getting his first job to advise on a golf course in his very early days, when the young man from Romford was only beginning to be recognized as a great player. Gradually more and more of this work came his way, particularly when he had grown older and so was more free from playing engagements. He had gifts that were very valuable to him for the purpose and in particular a visual memory for courses that was fully as remarkable as his accurate and tenacious memory for people and events. He could walk round a course which he had never seen before and then come in and draw plans of the holes with the bunkers, both as they were and as he wanted them to be. Such a memory must have served him well whenever he saw a fresh course, for it would enable him to call up what Sherlock Holmes called 'parallel instances.' The whole scheme of bunkering of some similar hole elsewhere would spring into his head and suggest an appropriate alteration. I should not say that he was very imaginative or subtle in the designing of a hole—and it is possible to be too subtle for ordinary human nature—but he had what the golf architect needs, a good eye for country and, as in everything that he touched, a temperate judgment and a fund of plain common sense. We hear a great deal of the contrast between the penal and strategic schools of architecture and I do not propose to become involved in any discussion on that thorny question. I do not think that James was deliberately penal in spotting bunkers here and there to catch each and all of the bad shots. He was much too good an artist for that, but at the same time he did not like to let the errant player 'get away with it,' and would now and again have a gently malign satisfaction in blocking his too wide and easy road.

One bunker of his comes instantly to mind, because it played its part in an historic disaster and was the subject of an historic comment by its victim. I have mentioned it before; it is that at the great fourth hole, the Pow Burn, at Prestwick. Those who knew the hole before 1918 will remember that there was a fair and ample strip of turf that curved with the curve of the burn, presenting the obvious line from the tee and affording the nearest and best position from which to play the second. In the middle of this inviting space James placed his bunker. He had not entirely blocked the road, for there was still room to squeeze through between the bunker and the burn, at once a narrow and a tempting enterprise. If the player could not face it he could safely pull away wide to the left, whence he could still reach the green with a considerably longer shot. In short the hole offered what John Low called a 'contest of risks' and the player was left to take the bigger or the smaller risk—a fair though somewhat trying alternative.

I think that Taylor, who is a Dickens scholar, must have had in mind Scrooge's remark that the man who cried 'Merry Christmas' should be buried with a stake of holly through his heart. He, as will be remembered, wanted James buried at the bottom of his own bunker, his heart transfixed by a niblick. It was a savage wish though not an unnatural one, since that bunker went far to decide whether Taylor or Vardon should win a sixth championship. Yet I do not think that James was unduly venomous in placing that bunker. He left it to the player to take a risk in the hope of gaining an advantage, but left him to make this choice with his eyes open. That is the kind of problem that has to be faced at most if not all the great holes of the world.

James was by all accounts a very resolute architect in that once he had made up his mind he did not at all want his plan to be altered and disliked even the suggestion of any change. It was a curious fate that he should live and play for so many years of his life on two of the best of inland courses, the Old and the New at Walton Heath, and yet have little or no hand in the designing of them. After Herbert Fowler's death he would no doubt be consulted as to any change, but as long as Mr. Fowler was there, I doubt if anybody else had much say in the matter, for he was not only a most accomplished architect, with a touch of genius, but also an instinctive despot. So when people think of James as the architect of his own home course they are wrong. The most famous course with which his name is rightly connected is Gleneagles, where he is commemorated by a hole called Braid's Brawest. The too elaborate and alliterative Scotticism of some of the names there—the Denty Den, the Kittle Kink and so on—makes me, I confess, feel a little ill, but for Braid's Brawest I have a weakness and it is in my recollection a great hole, if not perhaps so fierce as when I first saw it. Then the course was still new and the turf had not been trampled hard and full of running by myriads of holiday-making feet. Certainly it was in those days a tremendous course, altogether too long for any but the lustiest hitters and seemed made to suit its mighty creator. It should be added, and I know James would have liked it said, that he had an able ally at Gleneagles in the late Major Cecil Hutchison, who afterwards did some admirable work as an architect on his own account.

Another fine course in Perthshire, Blairgowrie, owes much to James as, if I may so term him, a part-time parent. When it came to turning the old nine-hole course into one of eighteen and the taking in of new land in consequence, James was called in; he and Millar, the professional there, planned it out between them and without apportioning exact shares there is credit and to spare for both of them, for this is a lovely course. I have, alas, only been there once, when my powers of walking would not let me go all the way round, but from what I saw it remains in my head as one of the very best, as it is also one of the prettiest of inland courses, in a very select class indeed. It is probably like the impertinence of a Southerner to say so, but at the first sight of the Blairgowrie course he believes that he has been transported on a magic carpet to wake up in Surrey, very near Woking. The sandiness, the fir trees, the heather, the fairways bending their way this way and that—here is the kind of course that first swam into the ken of Southern golfers towards the end of the nineteenth century and made them realize that life could be worth living even away from the sea and near London. It may very well be that a golfer from Blairgowrie coming to Woking would say that it might almost, not quite of course but almost, be in Perthshire. Do not let me and that hypothetical patriot quarrel! Here at any rate is beautiful golfing material used with a real feeling for its beauty.

It was, I think, Gleneagles in particular that made James well known and sought after as an architect, so that in the years between the two wars work came to him in a steady stream. I had known he was kept busy but I had not fully realized how busy, until I heard from Mr. J. R. Stutt of Bournemouth who has very kindly helped me with information. His firm did the constructional work on a large number of courses from James's plans and he says that during the twenty years or so between wars, apart from numerous smaller jobs in the way of bunkering or altering, James had the designing of at least six to seven new or 'reconstructed' courses each year. He has given me a list of the more important courses to which James was called in and it is most impressive: Carnoustie; Dalmahoy; Blairgowrie; Royal Blackheath; Ramsey; Queen's Park, Bournemouth; Rhyl; Scarborough; Leamington Spa; Wildernesse; Buchanan Castle; Weir Park, Exeter; Arcot Hall, Newcastle; Truro; Belleisle, Ayr; Drayton Park, Birmingham; Kingswood; Finchley; Dunstable; Bangor, Co. Down; Mullingar; Howth; Waterford; Hilton Park, Glasgow; Milton Park, Peterborough; Torbay; Stover, Newton Abbot; Eaglescliffe, Co. Durham; Dawlish; Middlesbrough; Greenock; Welshpool; Oswestry; Forfar; Boat of Garten; Orsett. It is a wonderfully comprehensive list and might supply admirable material for a game of 'General Post.' Apparently he had many invitations to lay out courses on the Continent but these he declined, having more than enough to do at home, and being influenced a little perhaps at the back of his mind by the thoughts of that dreadful crossing. 'His plans,' says Mr. Stutt, 'were always crystal clear and definite, and it was very exceptional indeed for even minor alterations to be made during the carrying out of the work.' I may add that I have seen some of his plans myself and can confirm what Mr. Stutt says of their clarity and precision.

Chapter XII

A Man of Character

THE future golfing historian will doubtless perceive that during the lifetime of James Braid and his distinguished contemporaries the position of the golf professional became an altogether different one, alike in reward and in social status. It is not so certain whether he will appreciate how much that difference was due to their fine example in character and conduct. Unquestionably their chance came with the immense spread of the game in their time but it was by the way they took that chance that they showed themselves the men they were. The professional of their boyhood's days has been in many ways a good fellow enough, but his chances had been comparatively few and his temptations many. There were very few greens that needed or could afford a professional and so, unless he was one of the few lucky and resolute ones, he never rose far above the status of the caddie from which he had originally emerged, and when hard times or old age overtook him he ended as he had begun. If he was inclined to drink too much, as he often was, he was not greatly to be blamed, for his life produced naturally many idle hours and drink was one obvious way in which to pass them. If he were not always as self-respecting as he might have been, he led to some extent the life of a parasite with those who had more money than he had, and this is not one that tends to self-respect. He had had little education but this was not his fault. He was very often a good companion with a humorous turn to his tongue but, seriously regarded, he was not as a rule perhaps the best of citizens.

At the time when James and his contemporaries were emerging from boyhood the professional's opportunities were improving. In the later 'eighties when he was seventeen or eighteen the game was spreading like wildfire over England and the demand for someone who should combine the greenkeeper, the club-maker and the teacher was in consequence rapidly increasing. But even so it did not till a few years later offer a very inviting prospect and it is easy to understand how James's parents thought that a safe steady-going job as a joiner was a wiser investment than a plunge into the wild unknown England, where their lovable but reprehensible relation, Douglas Rolland, had taken sanctuary from the stern edicts of his native land.

By the time James had decided to take the plunge the prospects in England were perceptibly brighter, and not only there, for the game was likewise booming in Scotland. There was now a real chance for a steady man to make a decent living and, if he were an outstanding player, something more than that. But the margin of profit was still small and the player's rewards inconsiderable. To win a prize of £10 on the way to the Open Championship brought with it the comfortable assurance that at least the expenses of the visit were provided for. To be a good player was by no means enough; the professional must be ready to turn his hand to anything: mending a club one minute; rolling the green or if need be digging a new bunker the next; ruling as caddie master over a herd of boys. It was a hard and busy life and beyond all these multifarious duties the club professional must be ever ready to make himself pleasant to all sorts and conditions of members, most of them ready no doubt to be pleasant themselves, but a few of them exacting and unreasonable to an infuriating degree. All these difficult things James and his great contemporaries achieved in a truly remarkable degree; always dignified and always respectful; knowing their exact places and never outstepping them; utterly refusing to be spoiled—and there are always those ready to spoil professional game-players; steadily raising the whole status of their profession as they raised themselves; models of good and natural manners on and off the course. They set a wonderful example and the good they did will live long after them.

Apart from this universal esteem and respect felt for himself and his colleagues, James had a truly remarkable power of inspiring affection. This became more and more noteworthy in his later years, for we have as a nation a deep and genuine feeling for a grand old man in any walk of life and not least a grand old game-player. But throughout his career he had had the gift of making people fond of him. Up to a point it is not difficult for a prominent player of games to inspire personal liking, and it is perhaps easier for golfers than for the heroes of other games, since in the nature of their game they are surrounded and hemmed in by potential admirers, longing to repeat a single word overheard or, still better, to extract one addressed to themselves. To suffer them gladly is one of the tasks to which the Champion must school himself, and he must also learn, if he can, to make some pretence of remembering the man who said 'Well played' at the tenth hole on a course never visited before or since some dozen years ago. A golfer who, like the members of the Triumvirate, plays in the course of years at numberless different places must inevitably be in the position of having met for a flash of lightning thousands of people of whom he has not the faintest recollection. But they remember him vividly, often crediting themselves with a familiarity with the great man which is wholly illusory, and retailing the mildest of small stories of what he said or did. Even as the Duke of Wellington was 'much exposed to authors' so James was much exposed to spectators of this kind and nobody was better qualified to deal with them. His invincible tranquillity made him endure their untimely interruptions and his memory was such that he sometimes did, contrary to all the laws of probability, really remember them.

These qualities naturally made for a general liking, but such a popularity as almost any Champion can command, is very different from the real, deep affection that not only his friends but thousands who had barely exchanged a word with him felt for James. His was not merely that negative popularity such as is sometimes gained by silent and reserved men. James was beyond all doubt reserved, almost to a point of being secretive; he did not like garrulous people; he said very little and could hardly ever be said to let himself go. He certainly never seemed to go out of his way to seek affection, and if he felt it for others, as I am convinced he did, I doubt if he ever expressed it in words. He might have felt it altogether too gushing and barely decent to do so; yet it was an essentially positive affection that innumerable people felt for him and one that grew ever warmer with the years.

The other day when I re-read yet once more *The Strange Case of Dr. Jekyll and Mr. Hyde*, one familiar sentence struck me as almost exactly applicable to James. It describes Mr. Utterson the lawyer, an austere rugged man, 'backward in sentiment,' silent and undemonstrative. 'At friendly meetings, and when the wine was to his taste, something eminently human beaconed from his eye; something indeed which never found its way into his talk, but which spoke not only in those silent symbols of the after dinner face, but more often and loudly in the acts of his life.' There was something eminently human about James, which made him comfortable company, even though he said little. And it was reinforced by a sly twinkle of humour which consisted often in no more than his obvious appreciation of something absurd which needed no putting into words, but now and again gave a dryly amusing and even a caustic twist to his tongue. It is not easy to give examples and certainly none would come from any of the public utterances that were now and again extracted from him, for he hated having to make speeches and discarded the few notes that he had painfully made beforehand, to relapse as soon as he could into silence.

Here is one little story, full of that pleasant twinkle, which I owe to his elder son James. 'When I was living in Cheshire from 1927 until 1939 we used to telephone to each other every Sunday evening after seven o'clock, and on one occasion during a particular week when the Lucifer Golfing Society's dinner had been held, and the then Prince of Wales was present, a certain paper stated that sitting next to him was Mr. James Braid, the famous golfer. My wife remarked when telephoning the following Sunday that she had noticed this. My father replied, "Oh no, the Prince of Wales was sitting next to me."

Another little remark of his that comes back to me, seems agreeably typical. A golfing society was holding its annual meeting at Walton Heath and a firm of ball-makers with a view to advertisement had sent to James as their almoner a present of two balls apiece for each player. Somebody hearing of this said facetiously to James that it must be very bad for business. 'Oh no,' he replied, with the ghost of a chuckle, 'I give them on the first tee.' There is a truly delightful humour—is pawky the right Scottish word for it?—in letting the players acquire their ammunition in the shop before receiving this handsome and unexpected supply at the starting point. It was the kind of canny little joke that appealed to him.

'Do you think I ought to get one of these wedges?' a distinguished visitor asked him in the last few months of his life. 'If you are thinking of buying it from me,' was the answer, 'I should say yes.' It was the kind of joke that he could well afford to make, for though he was essentially careful about money he was also intensely generous. I am sure he did many kind things of which very few have any knowledge at all and which were very likely unknown to any save the recipients. I do know that hearing a certain young professional had been in ill health and so been having a hard time he at once sent him a substantial cheque. I know too that he more than once helped young professionals, when starting on their own account, by lending them money to stock their shops. He was an essentially hospitable man, never wanting to receive without giving, always anxious to repay the friendliness of others, so hospitable indeed as to be difficult and indeed sometimes impossible to resist.

James was a monument of two invaluable qualities, common sense and discretion. It is impossible to think of his doing or saying a foolish thing and though he heard much he revealed nothing. Lord Riddell left him a legacy 'for his discretion' and the word was well chosen. If, as has been said, 'philosophy is nothing but discretion,' then James was well worthy to be called a philosopher. Moreover he had more than common sense, he had wisdom. I think that on any problem of which he was by experience competent to judge he would have given as sound advice as it was possible to obtain. If he did not feel competent, nothing would have induced him to say a word. 'His virtues walked their narrow round' but within that round there could not have been a more trustworthy counsellor, nor one who would think out a question more thoroughly before giving an opinion on it.

It may be said perhaps that the natural bent of his mind was cautious and conservative. He would look more than once before he leaped, and his first inclination was to say, 'I would not do it.' But there was about him this comforting and compensating quality that if his advice was in favour of doing it, whatever it was, it was pretty sure to be the right and wise thing to do. The very last words he spoke at a meeting of the Professional Golfers' Association almost immediately before going into the nursing home for his operation, were extremely characteristic of his restraining wisdom, 'Take care you don't cut your own throats.'

He had, as everybody must have, his likes and dislikes among people, but it would have taken an extraordinarily keen observer to guess at them from his calm, dignified, unchanging good manners. As

he was a generous man in his everyday life, so he was
a generous opponent at golf, and the same high
praise must be given to his illustrious adversaries.
They were constantly trying to beat one another
and for several years the highest honours were very
nearly confined to their small group. Each of them
wanted with his whole soul to win, for no one can
attain to such a position as was theirs without a
fierce desire for victory; but they remained mag-
nanimously equal to either fortune. It is not in human
nature never to feel some grievance against the Fates
in defeat and some envy of the victor, but whatever they felt they gave no sign of their emotions and
remained models of good losing as of good winning.

James was a very wise man rather than one of
intellectual interests. His reading apart from the
newspaper consisted almost exclusively of Wild West
and cowboy stories, such as are usually dear to the
schoolboy's heart. He would read the didactic works
on golf by his rivals and contemporaries, not, I judge,
with any passionate zest but rather in the dutiful
spirit which makes an intelligent man take an interest
in what concerns his own business. When such a
book was published, I am told he would keep it in
the shop and turn to it when there was for the moment
nothing to do. If he was critical of the doctrines
propounded there I doubt if he was ever heard to
say so. It was one of the strongest parts of his
discretion that he was very chary of criticism. One
of his Wild West stories always accompanied him on
his journeys, but he never went to a cinema nor to a
theatre except to hear Harry Lauder of whom he
was a great admirer.

I have already tried to give some account of
James's everyday life at Walton when he was still in

his prime as a player. Naturally it changed to some extent as the years crept on and he ceased to play in tournaments, except for his visit once a year to the Championship. Yet perhaps it changed less than might have been expected. He still made a good many journeys away from home though he now went to design courses rather than to play on them. One great change indeed there was in his life, for in March 1939 Mrs. Braid died. She had never seen James play in a competition but during the Championship would sit at her bedroom window watching for a messenger from the shop to bring the news. When he won his last two Championships he had been met by the elder of his two boys at Tadworth and driven home in an open carriage amid the cheers of the villagers.

They had already had a housekeeper for a year or two before Mrs. Braid's death and she stayed on to look after James. Except during the Second War when there was naturally less golf at Walton and he felt a heavier responsibility for the course, there was no profound alteration in his life from day to day. Naturally as the years went on he played less golf, but he played as much as he could and he rather grudged the time spent in other ways. Will Brown has told me one eloquent and touching little story of James's devotion to the game. When there was snow on the ground and it was palpably impossible to play he would grow very restless. Every now and again he would get up and go outside the shop for a minute or two. Nothing was said but everybody knew he had gone out to look hopefully for signs of a thaw. 'If he had got over this last illness,' Brown added, 'he would have played golf till he could not walk any more.' It is by the way pleasant to know that Brown was invariably the first man to enter James's house at exactly one minute past twelve on New Year's Day, since James like a good Scotsman always saw the New Year in.

As he grew older James grew in many ways even more of a personage in the golfing world. It is the custom of the Professional Golfers' Association that the Open Champion of the year should be its Captain. James had therefore naturally held the office in his five years as Champion. In 1946 the Championship was won by an American professional, Sam Snead, and since he could not hold office, the P.G.A., as I mentioned before, made James captain yet again for the ensuing year. He was not only an honorary member of Walton Heath but a director of and shareholder in the club. He was the only honorary member of the Parliamentary Golfing Society.

And then in the last autumn of his life came a unique honour for a professional golfer, when he and J. H. Taylor and Willie Auchterlonie were elected honorary members of the Royal and Ancient Club. This gave him the most genuine and intense pleasure and it was truly sad that he could not revisit the club as a member and receive the warm welcome that awaited him there. He said, as was his wont, comparatively little about it, and indeed all his honours and the ever-growing respect paid him had not the slightest apparent effect on him. That self-respecting modesty, which had always marked him and his famous contemporaries, remained wholly unchanged. He was a director of the Walton Heath club but he was also, as he always had been, its servant and it was thus he primarily regarded himself.

Though he was constantly in the club house he scarcely ever used the front door but came in at the back. He lunched there every day but always in the Secretary's room and never in the club dining-room, where his picture hangs, unless he was specially asked there. On a Sunday in particular he never went into the dining-room. To go to the bar alone was a thing it would never have occurred to him to do. As he always had done, he waited to be asked. It was part of his innate good breeding that nothing could make him alter the line of conduct which he had marked out for himself and which came naturally to him.

In the evening he would often go across the road from his house to the social club in Walton founded by Lord Riddell, of which he was an original member. Here he would occasionally play darts but his more regular game was billiards. A great player he was not but he drove the balls about the table with much of that 'divine fury' which Horace Hutchinson had attributed to him so many years before, sometimes with results very disconcerting to the opposition.

The club never taught him to smoke. He had given it a very brief trial in his youth and decided firmly against it. His life at home remained in many ways as it always had been. Though he made so many journeys he would never have a car, but stuck to a train, not on economic grounds but because he was always prone to car sickness. He also refused to have a telephone and that was probably an example of his natural shrewdness; he knew that he would be given too little peace if he had it.

I suppose the thought of retiring must now and then inevitably have occurred to him but only as an ulti-mate and distant possibility. When the reporters asked him on his eightieth birthday whether he meant to retire he entirely and, I am convinced, genuinely denied it. Why should he retire? He loved

his work and the play that was part of it. Whenever
there was a competition at Walton Heath he was
there to start the players and if need be to help manage
the crowd. When the *Daily Mail* tournament was
played there during the last summer of his life I saw
him positively run, not very far and not very fast, but
still run to shoo away an intrusive onlooker. He
would have been lost without his life's work and it
ought perhaps to be a cause for thankfulness that he
never had to endure life without it.

CHAPTER XIII

The Last Year

As the 6th of February 1950 drew near, the golfing world awoke to the almost incredible fact that on that day James would be eighty years old. There had been annual warnings of it, since each year we had been told how in his birthday round he had achieved a score lower than the total of his years. Still he was so palpably young and active that the fourscore years seemed unbelievable. The great day broke wet, cold and windy, the kind of day that sees Walton Heath at its fiercest and bleakest, but James never dreamed of not playing and went out well wrapped up in mackintoshes to face the photographers on the first tee. He just and only just failed on this occasion to beat the years. The wind was so strong that, as he told me that evening at dinner, he had no hope of carrying the cross-bunker and reaching the last green in two, and even when James was eighty that meant a wind indeed. His third was just caught in the side bunker and in the end he holed out in 81.

He was not a penny the worse of his buffeting and came up in the evening to a small dinner given by some friends of his at the Golfers' Club, to which I had the very pleasant honour of being asked. I sat next to him and recall the gently despairing gesture with which he pulled himself to his feet to return thanks for the toast of his health.

Later on in the year there was another and larger

dinner at Walton when a presentation was made to him. Sir Frederick Hamilton was to have presided but was unfortunately not well enough to be there. However, the Chairman read the words that he had meant to say, and they so well express what everybody there must have felt that they are here set down.

'Only extreme physical weakness would have prevented me paying my personal tribute to my old friend and our distinguished fellow-member, James Braid.

'Braid has of course been a very great golfer—one of the greatest in his day. Five times Open Champion; four times winner of the *News of the World* competition; once Open Champion of France; the record speaks for itself. But it is not because he is a great golfer that on the occasion of his eightieth birthday the other day he was acclaimed wherever golf is played—that is throughout the really civilized world—as indisputably the Grand Old Man of the game. It is rather because of a rare combination of qualities which would have made him a great personality at any time and in any sphere of life.

'His association with Walton Heath has covered the whole life of the Club and the most active part of his career. For forty-six of the most momentous years in history, he has been our guide, philosopher and friend, and it is safe to say that as the years went on he more and more attracted not merely the regard and esteem but the affection of fresh generations of members. In its earlier days the Club had a very large membership of distinguished politicians and journalists. Braid recalls one morning when the Prime Minister and three other Cabinet Ministers together with five outstanding journalists or newspaper proprietors were gathered together with their caddies on the first tee waiting to drive off. He will tell you that he has always regarded Mr. Winston Churchill as the authentic inventor of the "greensome." Mr. Churchill was never a distinguished exponent of the game, but in those days it was almost necessary, if you wanted to be in touch with the latest political movement, to play golf at Walton Heath and by selecting Braid as his partner, Mr. Churchill was able to get the maximum exercise and win a fair proportion of matches, while not unduly hampering the efforts of the other players. Against this brilliant background Braid moved easily, always a distinctive and indeed a distinguished figure in his own right.

'During the Second World War Braid to many of us seemed to stand for a certain continuity and stability in human affairs and in a world of change to symbolize the unchanging values. During that period it so happened that owing to the exigencies of war, I was for a considerable time as Chairman of the Club left with a large amount of responsibility. My own personal debt to him is immense, and I can testify better perhaps than any one else how much the Club owes to the sagacity of his judgment and his devotion to its interests.

'When Bismarck was being congratulated on his eightieth birthday he replied, "You can take it from me that the first eighty years of a man's life are the best." Speaking from five years' experience I can say that although this is to a large extent true, it is by no means the whole truth. For one thing octogenarians realize that a man's real wealth is calculated not merely by his banking account, but by the number and quality of his friends. In that respect our dear old friend James is well· in the millionaire class. Long may he flourish, long may he beat the number of his years when he goes round the course on his birthday. With all my heart I say many happy and healthy returns.'

Lord Simon was also called upon to say something in praise of James. He said that if the College of Heralds were called upon to devise a coat of arms for him, his shield would surely be emblazoned with a 'royal tigre proper on a field vert with supporters in the form of coneys cherchant in a warren,' or in plain English 'a right royal tiger, who always kept on the "pretty," surrounded by rabbits looking for their balls in the rough.' 'Braid,' Lord Simon added, 'is indeed the embodiment of what every golfer should wish to be, both on the links and off them. His wisdom, his gentle temper, his modesty and his perfect courtesy to everyone, have made him the most beloved, as well as the most admired figure in the game.'

I have also a copy of what James at any rate meant to say. Whether he exactly carried out his intentions I am not sure, but I am told that he made 'a charming little speech.' Here is his draft:

'Words fail me on this occasion and although it is becoming the fashion for orators to become golfers, it does not follow that golfers can become orators, and it is easier to me to pitch the rubber-core than to pitch a tale. I need hardly say I am most grateful and proud to be thus honoured by the members of the Walton Heath Golf Club and other friends on this occasion of my birthday, who have helped to subscribe towards this most beautiful salver and cheque. I have been a fairly lucky man since I came to Walton Heath Golf Club. I was in at the beginning of the Club and have seen it grow into one of the leading Clubs in the country. It has been my pleasure

and privilege to attend to the wants of the Members
for a long time now and I hope to do so for some
time longer.

'I may say that it is a long time since I started
golf and hope to play a bit longer. There have been
lots of changes in the game since I started, both in
dress and implements and conditions of the courses.

'It isn't often I've seen so many Club Members
together. It takes me back to my own early days
when the Open Championship was a real meeting.
Everybody stayed in one little area and got to know
one another a lot better; nowadays the cars whisk
everybody away and one half of the players don't
know the other half.

'Thank you all again, Ladies and Gentlemen.'

The great occasion over, life returned once more
to its steady jogtrot and its regular rounds of golf. If
there was any change to be noticed in him with the
gliding of the year, it was, as his son Harry has told
me, that he was rather more inclined to talk and tell
a very occasional story of the past. I remember
meeting him at the Old Deer Park when he asked me
if I had seen a certain young amateur of great promise
drive. It was a small thing and yet I remember
thinking that once upon a time he would hardly have
volunteered so much; he was getting relatively
voluble.

He took part during this last summer in one agreeable little ceremony. There was given to the
Engineering Golfing Society a small statuette of
James, addressing the ball for a run-up shot. It was
to be a prize for a competition in which the handi-
capping was done strictly on the basis of age, each
player subtracting the number of his years from that
of his strokes. How impossible would have been the

task of all the other players if James himself could have been a competitor and taken 80 off his score so as to produce in all human probability a minus total. He came over to Woking where the Society's meeting was held, spent a friendly afternoon, and presented the prize to the winner. Journeys were nothing to James, especially journeys to Scotland, and he was at the Open Championship at Troon to watch at least one day's play. I suppose there was not a soul in the big crowd that did not recognize that characteristic figure. He was becoming almost as well known by sight as had been W. G. I remember that he was supposed to be coming to tea at the hospitable house in which I was staying, but he was still, I think, a little on his guard against parties and to our disappointment he had softly vanished away. I only saw him once after that for a moment at a Memorial Service to Lord Wardington, when he seemed perfectly well and indeed I believe he was well to all outward appearances, until it was decided in November that it was necessary for him to have an operation. The two last rounds of golf that he ever played on his beloved Walton were both low in the 70's and immediately before going into the nursing home he went to a P.G.A. meeting and gave as ever some very sage and temperate advice. The operation seemed to have been successful and all was going so well that his friends heard that he would soon be home again. Then the news became disquieting; there came a set-back and in two days it was all over. He died on November 27th and was buried at St. Peter's Church at Walton-on-the-Hill. Later there was held a Memorial Service in a London church at which there was a notable assembly of his golfing friends and brother professionals.

There is one point which after some little hesitation I think right to mention, one which I should normally regard as wholly private. James, as was in the ordinary course published in the newspapers, died intestate and many people wondered audibly, for I have heard them, how so careful and so generous a man should have done so. It should therefore be known that before he went into the nursing home he had written down exactly what he wanted done and had remembered those who had worked with him in the shop and in the club. He had in effect made a will but it had not been formally completed or witnessed. All the desires that he had thus expressed were carried out by his family and there was one of particular public interest, namely, that the medal given him by the Royal and Ancient Club as the winner of the Open Championship in its jubilee year, 1910, at St. Andrews, should be given back to the Club. It is pleasant to think that the Club will thus possess for ever this memorial of an honorary member than whom none has been more universally honoured.

On June 1st, 1951, the plaque to James's memory was unveiled at Elie by Mr. Henderson Stewart, M.P. Lord Simon, who has had a house at Walton Heath for many years, has very kindly given me a copy of the letter which he had written to Mr. Henderson Stewart who read it aloud at the ceremony: 'I am much interested to know that you are unveiling a tablet to the memory of James Braid on the house in Elie where he was born. I remember well going over from St. Andrews a few years ago to Elie, when the place was pointed out to me and I felt like a worshipper who had gone on a pilgrimage.

'It was my happiness to know Mr. Braid well for

many years, as my country house is close to Walton
Heath, where, in the course of his service as professional there, he did every hole on both courses at
some time or other in 2, and on his eightieth birthday
went round in 81. Many is the time that he has
given me a golf lesson. For his character and
personality, I shall always preserve a deep admiration,
nay, a real affection. He had the dignity and gentle-
ness which sometimes show themselves in a great man
who is master of his craft, but who feels nothing but
sympathy and interest in others much less skilled.
He was incapable, I believe, of any unkind word and
every golfer who knew him loved him. When I
made a bad drive, the worst he would say was "Tut,
tut, tut, I'd no swear that ye *looked* at that one."
And if I hit the majority of a dozen practice shots
more or less as he approved, while making a dreadful
mess of the rest of them, he would say at the end, with
a kindly waggle of his finger, "Weel, now, I'd say
that *on the whole* that was verra guid." To my mind
James Braid was a perfect example of what the kingdom of Fife can produce and I envy you the privilege
of taking part in the ceremony on Friday.'
    On James's death many other tributes both
technical and personal were paid to him, but the two
from which I should like to quote were written in his
lifetime by two of the most distinguished of his brother
professionals of different generations. First comes his
friend and rival for years J. H. Taylor, in his autobiography *Golf: My Life's Work*. It is technically
interesting as an opinion of James's play by one best
qualified to give it, and at the same time is eloquent
of an old friend's affection. I begin my quotation
when J. H. is speaking of James's 'break through'
and his winning his first Championship. 'In the next

year Braid's play became as irresistible as was Vardon's in his most polished period. As a hitter of the ball James has had no superior, and as a player up to the hole with any kind of iron club he challenges comparison with the best, and there could have been but very few who would dare demand a trial. Long, straight, beautifully controlled driving, with rasping and ripping iron shots were to be expected, but great as are their aids to successful golf, it was his putting that placed him in his proud position. Like others who at some time have found themselves labelled weak in a particular stroke, James has had tacked on to him the reputation of a bad putter. This may have been justified in the early days when he was gathering the threads of his game together and showed weakness when it was a matter of knocking the ball into the hole from short distances, a weakness that afflicts all. I suppose it is ludicrous to see a golfer who can consistently hit the ball long, straight distances and play up to the hole with precision, fail to hole the testing "yarders," but it is the critics who presumably see the funny side and who make the greatest error. I will agree, and I put it forward with diffidence and fear, that James has always been frightened by the short putt—what golfer that ever lived hasn't?—but when saying this assert with every confidence that this supposed weakness is more than compensated by the exactitude of the long, run-up approach putts. As a diviner of the true line to the hole there is no superior; and I am equally certain that as a judge of strength, that always tantalizing factor, he is in the front rank. James's rise to eminence in the putting game began when he first used an aluminium putter and discarded the weird and wonderful iron implements that all shaky holers-out fly to use as a hoped-for correction. Instead of a snappy, jerky action he developed a smooth, slow take-back of the club and stroked rather than hit the ball towards the hole. His success engendered a great confidence which increased until he became one of the world's finest putters, and I have yet to meet the player who could hole the ten-yard putts with greater regularity. Like myself, Braid has always suffered from the handicap of weak sight, and, until this had weakened so badly, James remained more than a dependable wielder of the shortest club in the pack. With his mastery over the longer and more robust shots, a mastery that was always assured and helped by his improved putting, it is no wonder that Braid became one to be held in the deepest respect. . . . Yes, indeed, James Braid had certainly made up for his late start. Jimmy will, I know, forgive me if I attempt a little character sketch which very long years of acquaintanceship may warrant. I do it in very few words, because he hates verbosity. This lovable character can be summed up in three— sincerity, trustworthiness, loyalty. Could I think of anything more fitting I would give it as a tribute to one of my dearest friends. James is a man of few words. His reticence is but a cloak to hide his real feelings.'

And now I should like to quote from another great golfer, thirty-seven years younger than James, who came to know him well and appreciate his many fine qualities, Henry Cotton. What follows is from his book *This Game of Golf* published some two years before James's death. 'I always believe that common sense is as necessary in golf as in other walks of life, and James Braid was clearly born with more than his share. This tall, stooping, ruddy-complexioned old

Scot is one of the wonders of the golfing world. Despite his years, his recent golfing exploits seem to increase his fame, for the older he gets the easier it seems to become for him to go round "in his age." He beats his age by an ever-increasing margin: at seventy-eight he celebrated his birthday with a 74. I write in 1948 and he still plays a round every day it is fine, on occasions going round twice—and he was born in 1870.

'Like J. H. Taylor and Harry Vardon, Jimmy, as I grew to call him as I gained my position in the golfing world, was of another era, and I knew his golf only when he was past his prime; yet it could easily be seen how great he must have been. What strikes me most about "Old Jimmy" is that although he has travelled less outside the British Isles than any other Champion (he has never crossed the Atlantic) he is as well known the world over as any golfing figure, to everyone, except possibly to the person in the following story. An American went to play at Walton Heath for the first time. There was no one in the club house to play with, so the Secretary suggested taking out Braid. It clearly did not register with the visitor who Braid was, but they played and Jimmy gave him "the works," much to the American's surprise. When asked later how he liked the course he said he had enjoyed it very much, but was amazed at "the golf the old fellow in the tin hut put up," adding that he must have been some "shooter" in his young days.

'Jimmy, besides being a great golfer from a technical point of view, is the possessor of a wonderful temperament and he learned never to show any emotion in his golf, and in addition is a man of very few words. I have only heard him make a speech in public on one occasion, and that was to say about half a dozen words at the presentation and dinner to J. H. Taylor, given at the Royal Mid-Surrey Golf Club in 1946 on his retirement.

'Jimmy loves Walton Heath and he has helped to make the courses there really great. He has a great eye for a golf hole and will cross a tract of virgin land and plot out golf holes as well as any man. He has been a successful golf architect, and his many courses are not rubber-stamped; they are original. . . . The amount of love Jimmy has for the game is difficult to guess from his expression, for whenever you see him plodding along during a friendly game, you would think he had been forced to go round, yet as he is financially independent, it can be assumed and rightly so, that he enjoys every minute he is playing. If it were not so, then many years ago we would have been deprived of his presence on the course, for the only need Jimmy has to go on playing is to give himself pleasure, or maybe, he realizes the pleasure he is giving to others.'

With those two tributes from great golfers of different generations I think I must draw this sketch to a close. I am keenly conscious of its imperfections. Some readers may complain that there is too much golf in it. To them I must reply that this was inevitable, since golf was James's life. Others, insatiable for statistics, may possibly think there is too little. James played so long and in so many matches and competitions that the book could have been almost infinitely swollen; but even golf can become monotonous. Allan Robertson, after a long series of rounds for several consecutive days, remarked that 'he had never had sic a bellyful o' gowf in all his days.' I did not want the reader to be conscious of such a surfeit and so deliberately left out all but the most important of the thousands upon thousands of rounds that James must have played.

As to the man himself, apart from his game, as far as the two can be separated, I think everyone that knew him recognized in James the same lovable qualities, modesty, dignity, reticence, wisdom and a deep and essential kindliness. On these all would agree. But I think there is another epithet that would come to most people's minds. They would call him almost instinctively a great man. Is there anything inappropriate in applying the word to one whose life was largely spent in playing a game? I do not think there is. 'Great' is one of those adjectives which we are unable to define, and if we are wise, we shall resolutely decline to try. We know what we mean by it; we naturally and unhesitatingly apply it to some people and James was one of them.

There is one other point which has struck me most forcibly over and over again when trying to write this book. I have emphasized it already but I do so once again at the end. I believe James loved golf with an intense, whole-hearted love the capacity for which, whatever its object, is not given to many people. He loved not merely the playing of it but everything to do with it, certainly not the least the making of new courses and the mending of old ones. Although I thought I knew him fairly well I did not fully appreciate his real passion for golf till I talked to his sons and his closest friends. Henry Cotton has pointed out in the passage I quoted that from seeing him play it would have been hard to tell whether he was doing it for pleasure or merely as part of the day's work. He never would and perhaps never could have put into words what he felt for the game,

but the feeling went very deep.   When he had been a
boy at Earlsferry he had not skated or played football,
thinking every hour wasted that was not spent on the
links.   I fancy that at the bottom of his heart he
thought much the same when he was an old man at
Walton Heath.

INDEX

Aberdovey G.C., Merioneth, 57
Acton G.C., 113
Advanced Golf, 13, 18, 58, 92, 108, 146, 152, 156-7
Aldeburgh G.C., Suffolk, 81
Amateur Chamionship. *See* Championships
America, 72, 75, 130, 138, 139-40
American Open Championship. *See* Championships
Anderson, Jamie, 23-4, 25, 49
Arcot Hall (Benton Park G.C.), Newcastle, 163
Army and Navy Stores, 32, 33, 35, 37, 46
Auchterlonie, William, 20, 67, 174
Ayton, Laurence B., 126

Balfour, Arthur James, Earl of, 148
—, Leslie M., 14-15
Ball, John, 15, 17, 41, 75, 86, 120, 126, 129
—, Tom, 107, 115, 116-17, 118, 119, 120
Bangor G.C., Co. Down, 163
Barnes, James, 38
Barnton, Midlothian, 34
Beginnings of My Golf, The, 45
Beldam, G. W., 57, 58-9
Belleisle G.C., Ayr, 163
Berwick, John, 28
Beveridge, Harold W., 126
Bexhill G.C., 17
Blackheath G.C., 11, 69-70. *See also* Royal Blackheath G.C.
Blackwell, Edward, 39, 47
Blairgowrie G.C., Perth, 162-3
Bloxham, J., 142
Blyth, Arnold D., 39
Boat of Garten G.C., Inverness, 163
Bomboudiac, Baptiste, 110
Bonsor, Cosmo, 81
Bournemouth, 37, 163
Braid, Harry Muirfield (*son of* J. B.), 9, 30, 56, 133, 152, 181, 189
—, James (*father of* J. B.), 12, 25, 32

Braid, James, birth (6th Feb., 1870) and boyhood, 11-24; apprenticeship as joiner, 26; to St. Andrews as joiner (1889), 29; move to Edinburgh (1891), 30; to London (Army and Navy Stores) as clubmaker (1893), 32; first professional match, Limpsfield (1893), 35-6; entered Open Championship for first time, Sandwich (1894), 39; victory over J. H. Taylor, West Drayton (1895), 41; became professional at Romford G.C. (1896), 46; first success in score play, Romford (1896), 49; second entry for Open Championship, Muirfield (1896), 49-51; lost Open Championship, Hoylake, by a single putt (1897), 52-4; married to Minnie Alice Wright (1898), 56; won first Open Championship, Muirfield (1901), 63-7; became first Captain of London and Counties Professional Golfers' Association (1901), 71; played for Scotland *v.* England, beating H. Vardon, Prestwick (1903), 78; won first *News of the World* tournament to be held, Sunningdale (1903), 79-80; left Romford G.C. for Walton Heath G.C. (1904), 81; won Open Championship, St. Andrews (1905), 90-3; partnered A. Herd for Scotland *v.* England, losing to J. H. Taylor and H. Vardon (1905), 98-9; won Open Championship, Muirfield (1906), 99-101; played in French Open Championship, La Boulie (1907), 108; won *News of the World* tournament, Walton Heath (1911), 127; war work (1914-18), 133-4; won singles in first international match

191